Praise   s
the God of

Timothy George's book *Is the Father of Jesus the God of Muhammad?*
is a timely and much needed work to help Christians understand Islam,
its history, and its beliefs. More important, the book will help Christians
understand the cornerstone and distinctive doctrinal foundations of historic Christianity. Lucidly written and most insightful, George's volume
will be must reading for Christian leaders and laypersons alike as we
face the new global challenges of the twenty-first century.

—DAVID DOCKERY, PRESIDENT,
UNION UNIVERSITY

Dr. Timothy George's treatment of the question of the relationship of
the biblical and Islamic views of God is fair, clear, and characterized by
a deep understanding of and appreciation for the issues involved and the
radical differences between Muslim and biblical understandings. While
exhibiting a "holy tolerance" toward Islam, Dr. George stands four-
square for the uniqueness of biblical material regarding the deity of
Christ, the importance of the Trinity, and the importance of maintaining
these as foundational Christian distinctives. His is a much needed work
that is timely in its appearance and ought to be read with gratitude by
all evangelical Christians.

—ROBERT C. DOUGLAS,
PROFESSOR OF INTERCULTURAL STUDIES,
LINCOLN CHRISTIAN SEMINARY

This is a clear, concise, and highly readable introduction to Muslim
thought and practice. Timothy George tells the truth about how Christians have often sinned against Muslims, and he encourages us to live
with some mystery in our attempts to understand a religious system that
has both commonalities and significant differences with biblical faith.
But he also points us to the Crucified One who alone is mighty to save.
This is must reading for all thoughtful Christians who want to understand their Muslim neighbors better.

—RICHARD J. MOUW, PRESIDENT AND
PROFESSOR OF CHRISTIAN PHILOSOPHY,
FULLER THEOLOGICAL SEMINARY

Brilliant, balanced, and biblically sound. The most important book Christians can read right now in these challenging times.

—CHARLES COLSON, CHAIRMAN,
PRISON FELLOWSHIP MINISTRIES

Another treasure from Timothy George. This is an urgently needed examination of Islam, and more, a stunning portrait of our God—Father, Son, and Holy Spirit.

—LON ALLISON, DIRECTOR,
BILLY GRAHAM CENTER

This timely and illuminating volume not only gives us a useful survey of Islam's basic beliefs but also clearly identifies the major similarities and contrasts between historic Christianity and Islam. Avoiding the pitfalls of invective, oversimplification, and needless accommodation, Professor George examines Islam's origins and outlines the misunderstandings and conflicts that have often marked its relationship with Christianity. No informed Christian can afford to be without the information found in this helpful book.

—JOHN N. AKERS,
BILLY GRAHAM EVANGELISTIC ASSOCIATION

The September 11 events have been traumatic for both the West and the Muslim world. It has forced us all to seek to understand the causes and how we should understand Islam itself. Theology is fundamental to this understanding, for it is theology that has formed our worldviews, heightened our prejudices, and hindered meaningful communication between Muslims and Christians. Here is one great good that has emerged from the trauma—a humble, balanced, clear, and excellent theological statement that will help Christians to both establish their faith and share it meaningfully with Muslims. It may even help Muslims formulate a theology of their own that counteracts the strident, hate-laden propaganda of Islamists. It is a MUST for Christians seeking to understand recent events and face the future with a new confidence in the efficacy of the gospel of the Lord Jesus Christ.

—PATRICK JOHNSTONE,
OPERATION WORLD

UNDERSTANDING THE DIFFERENCES
BETWEEN CHRISTIANITY AND ISLAM

IS THE FATHER OF JESUS THE GOD OF MUHAMMAD?

— TIMOTHY GEORGE —

ZONDERVAN™

GRAND RAPIDS, MICHIGAN 49530 USA

ZONDERVAN™

Is the Father of Jesus the God of Muhammad?
Copyright © 2002 by Timothy George

Requests for information should be addressed to:
Zondervan, *Grand Rapids, Michigan 49530*

Library of Congress Cataloging-in-Publication Data

George, Timothy.
    Is the Father of Jesus the God of Muhammad? : understanding the differences
between Christianity and Islam / Timothy George.
       p. cm.
    Includes bibliographical references.
    ISBN 0-310-24748-9
    1. God.   2. Jesus Christ — Person and offices.   3. Christianity and other
religions — Islam.   4. Islam — Relations — Christianity.   I. Title.
    BT103 .G46 2002
    261.2'7 — dc21

                                                2002007165

Interior design by Beth Shagene

Printed in the United States of America

---

05 06 07 08 /❖ DC/ 10 9 8 7 6

For
Alyce Elizabeth

We shall not cease from exploration
And the end of all our exploring
Will be to arrive where we started
And know the place for the first time.

CONTENTS

PREFACE

Thomas Merton once wrote that "every moment in every event in every man's life on earth plants something in his soul."[1] The seed of this book was planted in my soul during my first visit to Jerusalem in 1970. Rising early one morning before dawn, I listened from my hotel window to the piercing, eerie sound of the muezzin (Muslim crier) as he repeated the daily call to prayer from one of the minarets high above Gethsemane. Later on, I discovered the meaning of the words I had heard spoken in Arabic that morning: "God is most great. God, there is none save he. Come ye to prayer. Come ye to the good." I could not help but think of another invitation given in that same city long ago: "Come unto me, all ye that labor and are heavy laden, and I will give you rest. I will give you peace. I will lead you to the good."

From that day on I have been intrigued by Islam and its relationship to the Christian faith. This book is an effort to understand some of the basic theological differences between these two faith traditions that together comprise more than 40 percent of the world's population. Jerusalem is a city sacred to both Christianity and Islam, as well as to Judaism. In the Holy Scriptures we are commanded to pray for the peace of Jerusalem. This book is written with that prayer in my heart. It is a prayer for true *shalom* and true *islam*—the peace of God, which is beyond our utmost understanding, a peace gained by neither bullets nor arguments but only through surrender, surrender to the One whose love was written in blood on a hill not far from that minaret one Friday in Jerusalem.

This book grew out of a talk I gave to the board of Prison Fellowship Ministries, a wonderful organization of worldwide impact with which I am pleased to be affiliated. An abbreviated version of chapter 3 has been published in *Christianity Today*.[2] I am grateful to several friends and colleagues who read early drafts of the manuscript and offered helpful suggestions. My administrative secretary, Amy Corbin, prepared the manuscript for press amidst her other pressing responsibilities at Beeson Divinity School.

Scripture quotations are taken primarily from the *New International Version*, although on occasion I've used different translations for particular texts. Likewise, as a rule, I've followed N. J. Dawood's translation of the Quran, which I regard as the most literate English rendering of this classic text.[3] At points, however, I've given a different translation where the context and sense of the passage seemed to require it. Readers should know that Muslims regard all translations of the Quran as mere interpretations lacking the authority of the Arabic original.

This book is dedicated to my daughter, Alyce Elizabeth, a young woman of great courage and bright promise.

TIMOTHY GEORGE
THE FEAST OF THE EPIPHANY 2002

INTRODUCTION

It was an unusually beautiful morning—September 11, 2001. I was in the kitchen, finishing my oatmeal and reviewing my notes for the sermon I was scheduled to preach in chapel that day. My assigned topic: the first two words of the Apostles' Creed—"I believe." The text I had chosen: the words of the desperate father in Mark 9:24—"Lord, I believe; help thou mine unbelief" (KJV).

I flipped on the television to catch a glimpse of the morning news, and then I saw it: the towering inferno billowing with smoke, the second plane crashing into the second tower, the president's announcement—"America is under attack!" Later that morning, I canceled my sermon. Instead of a sermon, our faculty and students gathered to pray and weep, to read the Scriptures, and to come together around the table of Communion to remember a body broken and blood poured out.

Much of the commentary after September 11 focused on the motivation of those who had turned airplanes into bombs and who had killed thousands of innocent civilians in the name of God. Words unfamiliar to most Americans were now heard daily on the evening news: *jihad, Islam, Taliban, Allah, Quran, fatwa, imam, ummah, Ramadan*. But there had been warnings. In 1990 Bernard Lewis published in *The Atlantic* his celebrated essay "The Roots of Muslim Rage." A few years later Harvard historian Samuel Huntington argued that the coming world conflict would be of an order altogether different from the great struggles of the twentieth century—not a contest between East and West or between North and South, but "a clash of civilizations." Chief among these competing civilizations, he said, are Europe/North America, with its roots in Christendom, and China/the Far East, with its Asian philosophy of life. Most aggressive and threatening of all, however, according to Huntington, is Islam based on the prophethood of Muhammad and the precepts of the Quran. It seemed to many that the predictions of Lewis and Huntington were being fulfilled in Osama bin Laden's summons to all Muslims to comply with God's order to kill the Americans and their allies.

Scholars will undoubtedly continue to debate these complex historical and geopolitical issues. For followers of Jesus Christ, however, an even more pressing concern exists: *How are we to understand Islam in light of the Christian faith?* This is not a new question, of course, but we are compelled to face it with a new urgency into today's world.

> *How are we to understand Islam in light of the Christian faith?*

This reality was driven home to me several weeks after the terrorist attacks in New York City and Washington, D.C. After I spoke to a suburban church near Chicago, Illinois, folks there wanted to know—How can we talk about Jesus with our Muslim neighbors? Do we worship the same God they worship? What do Muslims think about Jesus? Which beliefs do we share in common with Muslims, and where do we differ from them? How should we think and pray about the Christian mission to Muslims? If Islam is "a good and peaceful religion"—as George W. Bush (president of the United States) and others have repeatedly said—why are so many Christians persecuted and killed in Muslim countries because of their faith? This book will examine some of these questions in the light of the historic Christian faith.

In discussing the serious theological differences between Islam and Christianity, we must avoid angry condemnation of all Muslims on the one hand and a facile minimizing of Christian truth-claims on the other. It's all too easy to assume an air of superiority and characterize Islam as a wicked, heinous religion, but to do so only serves to reinforce the misunderstanding and mistrust acquired through centuries of polemic and bitter conflict. Few will be led to Jesus through this kind of attitude. We dare not mitigate the scandal of the cross, but sometimes what is scandalous is not the cross but we ourselves! This happens whenever we approach other persons with our evangelical guns "loaded for bear" rather than with the respect and forbearance we owe to all persons made in God's image. It also happens whenever we confuse the preaching of the gospel with the promotion of our particular culture. And it can happen whenever we ignore the methodology of Jesus himself, who listened before he talked and who kept on loving even when he and his message were rejected. We must never forget that "we do not preach ourselves, but Jesus Christ as Lord" (2 Corinthians 4:5).

We frequently quote the Great Commission in the version Matthew gives to us at the end of his gospel. But in John's gospel, Jesus commissioned the disciples by means of different words: "As my Father hath sent me," he said, "even so send I you" (John 20:21 KJV). All our efforts to share the good news of Jesus with others take place within that ellipsis: "As ... even so." In other words, there is a direct correlation between the *content* of the message we bear and the *spirit* and temper with which we bear it. The very verse that calls us to "always be prepared to give an answer" also tells us how this task is to be done, namely, "with gentleness and respect" (1 Peter 3:15).

A few years ago a prominent church leader made the headlines when he declared, "Almighty God does not hear the prayer of a Jew!" Taken at face value, this statement raises all kinds of questions: What is wrong with the Lord's auditory capacities? Has God gone partially deaf? Could he not hear the prayers of the Jewish Messiah Jesus? Rather than underscoring the sole sufficiency of Jesus Christ (which I believe was the real intention of the comment), the ugly tone of the statement led to religious sloganeering—a divisive pitting of "us good guys" against "them others." In asking whether the Father of Jesus is the God of Muhammad, we are not engaged in a kind of "my God's better than your God!" ballyhoo. The Christian gospel does not allow for this kind of swagger.

But there is another danger equally perilous, though more subtle, in our pluralistic postmodern culture, namely, that we may be seduced by a false ecumenism that relativizes all differences among faith perspectives and world religions. In reaction to the violence and distemper we see displayed in so-called fundamentalism (of whatever religious brand), many people are touting a kind of uncritical pluralism that would amalgamate divergent faith traditions into one single homogenized whole.

An early expression of this perspective appeared in a 1932 report published by a committee representing seven mainline American Protestant denominations. It declared that the task of the evangelist and missionary "is to see the best in other religions, to help the adherents of those religions to discover, or to rediscover, all that is best in their own traditions. . . . *The aim should not be conversion.* The ultimate aim . . . is the emergence of the various religions out of their isolation into a world fellowship in which each will find its appropriate place."[1]

W. E. Hocking, the principal author of this report, went on to say that what the world really needed was a universal generic religion, one not marked by "the staleness of ancient subjectivities." "God is in the world," he said, "but Buddha, Jesus, Muhammad are in their little private closets, and we should thank them but never return to them."[2]

Is it any surprise that the sending of missionaries from these denominations has dwindled to a trickle? Or that evangelism in those circles has become for many a dirty word not to be mentioned in polite company? Jean-Marie Gaudeul has written an interesting book about many Muslims who have become Christians.[3] He tells of one university-educated Muslim who professed faith in Jesus Christ. He was baptized after many years of honest searching for the truth. When this new believer in Jesus informed one of his Christian minister-friends about the decisive step he had taken, all the minister could say was, "You disappoint me." How sad! It's one thing to plead for a Christian witness that is respectful of others, relational in approach, and sensitive to cultural differences. It is something else altogether to think that the good news of eternal life in Jesus Christ isn't really worth sharing anymore!

Even if the pluralist model was deemed to be viable for other world religions, it could never be so for Christianity and Islam. For all their shared history and common ties—and there are many, as we shall see—there are nonetheless certain irreducible differences that cannot be easily plastered over in the name of a superficial niceness. That is, this cannot be done without sacrificing the identity of either one or the other. Yes, only in the light of basic shared verities can real differences be seen and appreciated. But to ignore the one in the interest of the other proves to be both dishonest and disrespectful.

> *"We implore you on Christ's behalf: Be reconciled to God."*

For the true believer in Jesus, dialogue and witness are not mutually exclusive activities. We can gladly acknowledge and give thanks to God for whatever is true, noble, right, pure, lovely, admirable, excellent, and praiseworthy—wherever we may find such things. And indeed we may find them in the most unexpected places, including many of the world's living religious traditions. Thankfully, God has not limited his "common grace" to the structures of the visible church or to the boundaries of historic Christendom. Christians, of all people, should be interested in all things human and humane. But at the same time, as emissaries of the crucified and risen Redeemer, we have a message to deliver to all persons everywhere of whatever religion, or of none: "We implore you on Christ's behalf: Be reconciled to God" (2 Corinthians 5:20).

Devout Muslims and faithful Christians alike seek an encounter with one another based on honesty, civility, and an uncompromised commitment to telling the truth both *to* one another and *about* one another. As Christians, of course, we must always speak the truth in love. For truth spoken without love—in harshness, anger, or arrogance—will, like a boomerang, return to the speaker with vengeance. But speak the truth we must. Simone Weil knew this very well. Her own torturous pathway to faith in Jesus Christ was marked by a hesitation and doubt that was both personal and theological. But in her little book *Waiting for God,* she broke through to a clarity that is almost shocking to read. "Christ," she wrote, "likes us to prefer truth to him because, before being Christ, he is truth. If one turns aside from him to go toward the truth, one will not go far before falling into his arms."[4]

This book is neither a primer on Muslim theology nor a contribution to interreligious dialogue. I write as a Christian for other Christians. I believe that the primary task for a Christian theologian is to build up the faith of believers, not to demolish the arguments of opponents. Nurture, not polemics, is our first calling, though this does not preclude our responsibility "to contend for the faith that was once for all entrusted to the saints" (Jude 3). If you are a Muslim reader of this book, I hope you will find your views presented accurately in accordance with the orthodox teachings of your tradition. If I have misunderstood or misstated these teachings, I welcome correction. Some Christians may be disappointed because this book is not a vigorous apologetic against Islam and its many controversial practices (treatment of women, polygamy, understanding of the state, and so forth). My focus is shaped by the question that serves as the title of the book. The *doctrine of God* is at the heart of both Islamic theology and Christian faith. All other issues, however important, are secondary and derivative.

I was first introduced to the study of Islam during my student days at Harvard University. My major professor there, George Huntston Williams, always intended to write a comprehensive history of the church titled *The New Testament People: An Ecumenical History of Christianity with Attention to Its Relation at All Important Nodal Points with Judaism and Islam*. Williams never completed his projected magnum opus. But he conveyed to me, and to all his students, a sense of God's providential guidance of his people through history—the mystery of the body of Christ extended throughout time as well as space. I am also deeply indebted to Bishop Kenneth Cragg, whom I have never met but whose many writings have been to me what the Quran says the New Testament is—"guidance and light" (5:46)—in understanding the faith of Islam. It is no exaggeration to say that, more than any other Christian scholar in recent times, Bishop Cragg has sought to understand and explain Islam sympathetically, from within as it were, while never forgetting his own identity and allegiance to the One who is the Way and the Truth and the Life. The Father of Jesus, as Bishop Cragg once said, is the God who encounters us, not alone from the throne of his majesty on high, but also from a garden called Gethsemane.

CHAPTER ONE

WHAT IS ISLAM?

To hold back from the fullest meeting with Muslims would be to refrain from the fullest discipleship to Christ. . . . Not to care about Islam would be not to care about Christ.

KENNETH CRAGG

How would you characterize someone who believes in the literal, verbal inspiration of Scripture, who holds that Jesus is God's virgin-born Messiah, that Jesus healed the sick, raised the dead, bodily ascended into heaven, and will one day return to do battle with the antichrist and in the end truly reign on earth? This person knows that Satan is alive and well on planet Earth, that angels and demons are real forces to be reckoned with, and that after death everyone on earth will go to one of two places—the burning fires of hell or the beautiful palaces of heaven. This individual does not believe in evolution, but believes that God created the world in six literal days. This person happens to be a teetotaler, is strongly pro-life, and is committed to traditional family values. Women are highly regarded in the religious community to which this person belongs, but they do not function as preachers and leaders there. This person is also deeply patriotic, regards pacifism as a weakness, deplores the separation of church and state, and believes that government (ideally) should enforce God's will in every area of society.

Do you recognize this person as a strict, conservative, Bible-believing Christian? Well, maybe. But he or she might just as well be a devout, conscientious Muslim! More than any two religious traditions on earth, Christianity and Islam share both striking similarities and radical differences. Historically, the relationship between Christians and Muslims has been strained at best. All too frequently it has been marked by bloodshed and violence. But there is a verse in the Quran that presents a helpful perspective. This verse tells Muslims, "You will surely find that the nearest in affection to those who believe are the ones who say, 'We are Christians'" (5:82). On this good note, we begin our brief overview of the world's second largest and fastest growing religious tradition.

Who Are Muslims?

Muslims are sometimes called Muhammadans, after the prophet Muhammad. He organized the first Muslim community, or *ummah*, in seventh-century Arabia, and through him the Quran was given to the world. But Muslims themselves take the word *Muhammadan* as an insult. For all their devotion to Muhammad, they regard him neither as divine nor as the founder of their religion. Muhammad did not claim to be sinless or perfect, and, unlike Jesus, he did not receive worship from other human beings.

Another word still found in most dictionaries is *Moslem*, the anglicized form of the Arabic *Muslim*. *Moslem* is also heard as a term of condescension that harks back to colonial times, a word coined by stodgy Westerners with stiff upper lips who found it difficult to make the *mu* sound!

More than one billion Muslims in the world are followers of Islam. The word *islam* literally means "submission" or "surrender." It comes from the Arabic root word *s-l-m*, which connotes peace in Semitic languages—as in the Hebrew greeting *shalom* or in the name of the holy city, *Jeru-salem*. We hear echoes of this same root word in the common everyday greetings of Muslims—

salamalek ("peace be with you)" and *bissalma* ("go in peace"). Muslims believe that the very word *islam*, as well as the way of life to which it points, was revealed by God himself in the Quran. Some eighty days before he died in A.D. 632, Muhammad received a final word of revelation. After warning Muslims not to eat pork or any animals that hadn't been slaughtered in a ritually pure manner (a kosherlike procedure called *halal*), God said to them, "This day I have perfected your religion for you and completed my favor to you. I have chosen Islam to be your faith" (5:3).

> *Islam refers to a life of total surrender and obedience to God.*

Islam, in its original meaning, then, refers to a life of total surrender and obedience to God—exactly the kind of complete commitment called for in the love-hymn Christians sing about Jesus:

All to Jesus I surrender,
All to Him I freely give....
All to Jesus I surrender,
Lord, I give myself to Thee....

Although Muhammad rediscovered this "straight path to God" (another description of Islam), Muslims believe that this kind of submissiveness has always been the true natural religion of human beings everywhere. This is an important point in understanding the contrasting views of salvation in Islam and Christianity—a theme to be discussed in chapter 6.

If Islam means surrender to the will of God, then a *Muslim* is one who has made this commitment. Who are Muslims? Where do they live? What languages do they speak? What religious duties are required of them?

Many people mistakenly think that most, if not all, Muslims are Arabs. Perhaps this is because so much attention is focused in the news media on the Israeli-Palestinian conflict in the Middle East and the fact that Muhammad himself was from Arabia.

Many are surprised to learn of the truly global reach of Islam. For example, some 200 million Muslims live in Indonesia alone—about the same number as live in all the Arab countries combined. There are more Muslims in China alone than there are Southern Baptists in the whole world. When we speak of Islam at the dawn of the twenty-first century, we refer to a world-encompassing faith that has a growing presence in every continent.

The "Abode of Islam" (as Muslims refer to the Islamic world) stretches from Morocco in the western part of North Africa to Indonesia and the Philippines in the Far East. It extends from Nigeria and Tanzania in sub-Saharan Africa to Kazakhstan and Uzbekistan in Central Asia. Within this vast sea of humanity, missiologists have identified five major blocs of people bound together by common cultural and language networks:[1]

- *Arabic*—This includes Saudi Arabia, with its Muslim holy cities of Mecca and Medina, as well as Iraq, Syria, Jordan, and the Palestinians in Israel, Gaza, and the West Bank. It also includes the Arabic peoples of Egypt and other North African countries.
- *Indo-Persian*—A complex assortment of peoples that includes the Kurds, many Afghans, the Tajiks of central Asia, and Urdu speakers in India and Pakistan, among others.
- *Turkish*—The Turks belong to the same language family as the Koreans. They include many people groups that live beyond the borders of modern-day Turkey. Among these are the Turkmen, Azeris, Uzbeks, Kirghiz, Kazakhs, and Uighurs.
- *Malay*—This bloc of peoples includes Muslims in Malaysia, Singapore, Indonesia, the Philippines, and other islands of the South Pacific.
- *African*—This group includes all the black peoples who live in African countries south of the Sahara Desert.

Within these five great families of Muslim peoples dwell many of the world's refugees. From Kosovo to Kabul, from Gaza to Bangladesh, millions of Muslims have been displaced by war, poverty, and plague. Although Muslim countries control two-thirds of the world's oil reserves, the bounty from this natural resource has not alleviated dire human needs in so much of the Islamic world. One indication of social ferment in this vast world is *urbanization.* In recent years huge Muslim metropolises have arisen as millions of peasants seeking to survive have crowded into Istanbul, Cairo, Algiers, Karachi, Khartoum, Teheran, Jakarta, and Islamabad. These great cities have also proven to be fertile soil for Muslim militants with their anti-Western and anti-Christian rhetoric. What is called Islamic fundamentalism is only one stream of a much larger phenomenon, namely, the recovery and reassertion of Islamic identity based on a return to the founding principles of the Muslim faith. This means applying *Sharia,* the law of God based on the Quran, to every aspect of life—to its social and political, as well as religious, dimensions.

One of the most striking religious trends during the latter third of the twentieth century was the movement of Muslims in large numbers to the West. Islam is now the second largest religion in Europe. It will soon surpass Judaism to claim that distinction in North America as well. There are more Muslims than Methodists in England—the home of John Wesley—and more Muslims than Episcopalians and Presbyterians combined in the United States. United Nations world populations studies project that by 2025 some 30 percent of earth's inhabitants will be Muslims—nearly one out of every three persons in the world.[2]

Today there are approximately seven million Muslims and more than 13,000 mosques in North America. Muslims were among the first slaves brought to this continent from Africa. In 1717, a group of "Arabic-speaking slaves who ate no pork and believed in Allah and Muhammad" arrived in the American colonies.[3] From these early beginnings, Islam has become a major force within the African-American community in North America. Elijah Muhammad served as the key figure in this development. Born Elijah Poole, he was the son of a Baptist preacher in Georgia who moved to Detroit in 1923. There he met W. D. Fard, the founder of a black separatist movement known as the "Lost-Found Nation of Islam in the Wilderness of North America." In

1935 Elijah Muhammad became the leader of this group, which has continued to grow despite its internal divisions and certain unorthodox teachings (such as Elijah's deification of Fard as Allah!).

Malcolm X remains the most prominent national leader to emerge from this movement. A brilliant thinker and fiery orator, he made a pilgrimage to Mecca shortly before his assassination in 1965. The *Autobiography of Malcolm X* has become an American literature classic and an introduction to Islam for many new converts. In recent years, Wallace Dean Muhammad, Elijah's son, has sought to more closely align this movement with international orthodox Islam. This approach was rejected by Louis Farrakhan, who has emerged as the most charismatic and controversial leader in the revived Nation of Islam. On October 6, 1995, he led the famous "Million Man March" in Washington, D.C. In addition to many Muslims, this event also attracted Christian participants who sympathized with Farrakhan's moral rigor and his call to discipline if not with his distinctive doctrinal beliefs.

> *Christians need to be well-informed about the Islamic religion.*

For all the success of these Black Muslim movements, however, the majority of Muslims in America are immigrants and their descendants. Beginning in 1875, they have come to these shores from all quarters of the Islamic world. They represent numerous ethnic and linguistic backgrounds, as well as diverse political traditions. Physicians, businessmen, automobile workers, university students, restaurateurs, technicians, and entrepreneurs, they are found in nearly every walk of life. Their cultural impact on American communities is noticeable. For instance, a newspaper reporter in Philadelphia, Pennsylvania, observed that "during the last twenty years . . . the number of Muslim families in the region has quadrupled, and the number of mosques in the city alone has quintupled to 30. Ten years ago, there were perhaps only one or two *halal* meat markets, which obey Islamic dietary rules; now there are at least 10. There was perhaps only one *halal* restaurant; now there are at least half a dozen."[4]

What this reporter observed ten years ago has become a major trend in all large cities, and even in some small towns, across the United States and Canada. The Muslim presence is felt in other ways as well. In June 1991, Siraj Wahaj, a black convert to Islam, became the first Muslim to deliver the daily prayer in the U.S. House of Representatives. Eight months later (February 1992) Wallace Dean Muhammad led the opening prayers in the United States Senate. Muslim chaplains now offer regular religious services for followers of Islam who serve in the United States armed forces. On September 15, 2001, when Dr. Billy Graham addressed a grieving nation from the National Cathedral in Washington, assisting him in this service of prayer and remembrance were Muslim imams, as well as Jewish rabbis, Christian ministers, and priests.

Muslim communities in North America are growing through conversion as well as immigration. The Muslim Student Association, which was organized in 1963, publishes a monthly journal titled *Islamic Horizons*. This journal aims to correct misconceptions about Islam and to convey the message of the Prophet Muhammad to non-Muslim students and faculty members. In a similar vein, the American Muslim Council, begun in 1990, works to give Muslims a voice on issues of ethics and public policy. Among other things, this group wants to counter the notion that American principles of morality and justice are based on the Judeo-Christian tradition alone. They favor the more inclusive idea of such values deriving from the Judeo-Christian-Muslim tradition.

For the foreseeable future, Muslims will certainly continue to become more a part of mainstream daily life in North America and Europe. This means that opportunities for both interfaith dialogue and Christian witness will increase. Rather than react with suspicion, fear, or apathy, Christians need to be well-informed about the Islamic religion and also to understand the distinctive teachings of their own Christian faith. Without this, how can we reach out with Christlike love and godly wisdom to our Muslim neighbors and friends? As a British evangelical leader said recently, "God was so concerned that Muslims hear the gospel that he has brought the mission fields to the churches."[5]

Five Pillars

Regardless of where Muslims come from or what language they speak, they hold certain beliefs in common, and certain distinctive practices set them apart from other religious groups. True enough, not all Muslims are consistent in their beliefs or devout in the practices of their faith. There are many nominal Muslims— just as there are many nominal Christians. In addition, throughout the Muslim world there is the phenomenon of *folk Islam,* a term that describes the worldview of many ordinary Muslims who accept magical beliefs and practices at variance with the formal facets of official Islam. In his fascinating book *The Unseen Face of Islam,* Bill Musk describes the world of popular Islam, with its veneration of saints, divinization rituals, and power encounters.[6] Still, however widely their practices may vary, there are certain basic tenets and religious duties all Muslims acknowledge as given by God. At the heart of the Muslim faith are the "Five Pillars" of Islam.

Shahada

This simple one-sentence confession of faith is the basis for everything Muslims teach and believe: "I bear witness and testify that there is no god but God [Allah] and Muhammad is the Messenger of God." The word for "messenger" in Arabic is *rasul.* It is sometimes translated "envoy," "prophet," or "apostle." *Rasul* refers to a special kind of prophet who has been divinely sent to promulgate the holy Law of God—the *Sharia.* Others before Muhammad had fulfilled this office—Adam, Abraham, Moses, David, Jesus. Muhammad was not the first of God's special messengers, but he is the last—the "seal of the prophets." In the final sermon he preached before he died, Muhammad declared that no prophet or apostle would come after him and that no new faith would be born after Islam. So basic is the *Shahada* to Muslim identity that it is literally sewn (in Arabic) on the national flag of Saudi Arabia. This simple far-reaching creed is also the gateway into Islam, which has no sacraments or priesthood and no right of initiation, such as baptism. To solemnly recite this confession of faith, with sincerity, in the presence of at least two witnesses in its Arabic original *(la ilaha illa Allah)*, is to become a Muslim.

This statement not only affirms the prophethood of Muhammad and the oneness of God, in reverse order, but it also makes an important negative statement that is central to all Muslim theology. There is "no god" but God. In affirming the one unique supreme and sovereign Creator-God, the *Shahada* rules out all other claimants to the status of divinity. It powerfully repudiates all pseudo-gods and would-be gods. The principle of divine unity *(tawhid)* excludes all idolatry. The worst sin imaginable, from the Muslim perspective, is to identify or associate something created with the Creator. This sin of "associating with God" is called

> *The worst sin imaginable is to identify or associate something created with the Creator.*

shirk in Arabic. Those who commit it are known as *mushrikun*. To be a *mushrik* is to attribute to something other than God the power, right, worship, knowledge, sovereignty, and majesty that properly belong to him alone.

The reciting of the *Shahada* serves as an expression of this submission to God. This is at the heart of true Islamic faith. The *Shahada* is whispered into the ears of a newborn child at birth. It is repeated throughout life in the daily round of required prayers. And it is said again over the body of a Muslim about to be buried. The *Shahada* is also a part of the daily call to prayer shouted for centuries from Muslim minarets around the world. That remarkable and well-traveled man of British letters, Rudyard Kipling, left his impression of hearing this chant in faraway India:

"Allahu akbar" ["Allah is most great"]—then a pause while another muezzin somewhere in the direction of the Golden Temple takes up the call: *"Allahu akbar."* Again and again, four times in all, and from the bedsteads a dozen men have risen up already. "I bear witness that there is no god but God." What a splendid cry it is, the proclamation of the creed that brings men out of their beds by scores at midnight! Once again he thunders through the same phrase, shaking with the vehemence of his voice: And then, far and near, the night rings with "Muhammad is the Apostle of God." It is as though he were flinging his defiance to the far-off horizon, where the summer lightning plays and leaps like a bared sword. . . . Christian churches may compromise with images and chapels where the unworthy or abashed can traffic with accessible saints. . . . Islam has but one pulpit and one stark affirmation—living or dying, only one—and where men have repeated that in red-hot belief through the centuries, the air still shakes to it.[7]

Salat

Five times a day—just before dawn, at noon, at midafternoon, just after sunset, and again sometime around midnight—the devout Muslim is required to bow down before God in the direction of the Great Mosque of Mecca. The word *mosque* (*masjid* in Arabic) means "place of prostration" or "house of prayer." Every mosque in the world has a niche in the wall called the *mihrab,* which points in the direction of Mecca, the holy city toward which all Muslims face as they pray. In the world in which Islam arose, one bowed abjectly in prostration in the presence of a great king or imperial sovereign. When Muslims bow in this way before Allah, they are acknowledging the sovereignty and majesty of God.

The theme of divine transcendence is undergirded by the ritual washing of the hands, face, and feet. This cleansing is done before beginning *Salat*—and preferably by using running water. The worshiper also uses a prayer mat to keep him free from contamination and to provide a sacred space for prostration. Islam has no holy day of rest comparable to the Jewish Sabbath or the Christian Sunday. But Friday is the day designated for congregational prayer in the mosque, which Muslim men (but not women) are obliged to attend. As part of their daily prayer requirement, Muslims recite the seven verses of the opening chapter of the Quran:

In the Name of God, the merciful Lord of mercy.
Praise be to God, the Lord of all being,
The merciful Lord of mercy,
Master of the Day of Judgment!
You alone we serve, and to You alone come we for aid.
Guide us in the straight path,
The path of those whom You have blessed,
Not of those against whom there is displeasure,
Nor of those who go astray.[8]

Zakat

Sometimes translated "poor tax" or "charity," *Zakat* refers to the obligatory almsgiving required of all devout Muslims. According to tradition, 2.5 percent of one's annual income must be given for *Zakat*. The Quran itself (9:60) indicates how these funds should be used: "Alms shall be only for the poor and the destitute, for those that are engaged in the management of alms and those whose hearts are sympathetic to the faith, for the freeing of slaves and debtors, for the advancement of God's cause, and for the traveler in need."

In addition to the required alms, Muslims can also give freewill offerings for the sake of the poor. This kind of generosity is encouraged in Islam. Muhammad himself was an orphan who grew up in poverty and never forgot the importance of caring for those in need.

The stewardship of a blessed life remains one of the major themes in the Quran: "Did he not find you an orphan and give you shelter? . . . Did he not find you poor and enrich you? Therefore do not wrong the orphan, nor chide away the beggar. But proclaim the goodness of your Lord" (93:6–11). On the other hand, a life of selfishness and disregard for others will lead inevitably to damnation. The Quran warns that each soul is the hostage of its own deeds. On the final day of judgment, "those on the right hand ... will ask the sinners: 'What has brought you into Hell?' They will reply: 'We never prayed, nor did we ever feed the destitute.'" (74:38–44).

Sawm

Ṣawm refers to the duty to participate in the annual fast that takes place each year during Ramadan, the ninth month in the Islamic calendar. Because the Muslim year is lunar, this fast can occur at various seasons of the year. The purpose of the fast is to cultivate discipline and self-control and to encourage contemplation on the meaning of true submission to the will of God. Fasting during Ramadan lasts from the first light of morning to the setting of the sun at night. During each day of the month, Muslims are expected to abstain completely from all food and drink (even the swallowing of spittle is forbidden). Sexual contact is also forbidden. The fast emphasizes the equality of all persons before God, as no one (except children, pregnant women, and those who are sick) is exempted from its requirements.

But why fast during Ramadan? Muslims believe that the angel Gabriel first revealed the Quran to Muhammad during this month. This event is referred to in the Quran itself and is celebrated each year during Ramadan on what is called "the Night of Destiny":

> In the month of Ramadan, the Quran was revealed, a book of guidance for mankind with proofs of guidance distinguishing right from wrong. Therefore whoever of you is present in that month let him fast. But he who is ill or on a journey shall fast a similar number of days later on. God desires your well-being, not your discomfort. He desires you to fast the whole month so that you may magnify God and render thanks to him for giving you his guidance.
>
> 2:185

Hajj

Hajj, the final pillar of Islam, is the famous pilgrimage to Mecca. Pilgrimage is a part of many religious traditions, including Christianity. As a young man, Jesus himself made a pilgrimage to Jerusalem with Joseph and Mary. Throughout the centuries many Christian pilgrims have visited the sacred sites of the Holy Land, as well as countless other places associated with martyrs, saints, and reformers. Every Muslim believer is expected to make the *Hajj* to Mecca at least once in a lifetime, unless prevented for reasons of health or financial need. In Malaysia, the first prize in a national lottery is an all-expense-paid *Hajj* to Mecca!

Muslims throughout the world pray toward Mecca every day. Once every year, during the twelfth Islamic month, some two million Muslims from every corner of the globe gather there to perform the various rituals associated with the pilgrimage. Why Mecca? It was there that Muhammad was born. It was also there that he cleansed the cube-shaped shrine called the *Kabah,* which formerly housed the many idols of Arabia. The *Kabah* was near the very spot, according to Muslim belief, where Abraham offered Ishmael—not Isaac, as the Bible says. At the last moment God provided a substituted animal to die in the place of Ishmael. Significantly, the rituals of *Hajj* still include a literal sacrificing of animals, although most Muslim scholars deny that this act has any expiatory significance. There is no place for atonement or redemption in the Islamic understanding of salvation. Some Muslims believe that every step taken toward Mecca in the course of the pilgrimage blots out a sin committed in the past, while to die en route is to be included in the number of the martyrs.

The Role of the Prophet

The question Jesus once asked others about himself—"What do you think about the Christ? Whose son is he?" (Matthew 22:47)—must also be asked from a different point of view of everyone who studies the central figure in the rise of Islam: "What do you think about Muhammad? Whose prophet is he?" From the standpoint of comparative theology, Jesus and Muhammad are not really comparable in this way. For Muslims, Jesus is the virgin-born miracle-working Messiah and prophet of God, but not the divine Son of God. Christians, they think, are guilty of the worst kind of *shirk* because they attribute divinity to Jesus, Mary's son. Muslims believe that Jesus was "no more than a servant on whom we bestowed favor," as the Quran quotes God as saying (43:59). No Muslim would think of assigning divine status to Muhammad. It is not the Prophet but the Quran itself that holds a similar place in Islam to that of Jesus Christ in Christianity. The key difference is this: According to the Bible, the eternal Word of God was made *flesh* and lived on earth as a Jewish peasant named Jesus; for Muslims, the eternal Word of God was made *text* in the holy Quran revealed to Muhammad.

> No *Muslim* would think of assigning divine status to Muhammad.

From another perspective, however, it is impossible not to compare Jesus and Muhammad, for—despite the radically different roles they play in the two religions—they are the key historical figures whose life and work marked a new beginning for Christianity and Islam, respectively. The *Shahada* itself irrevocably links the confession of the one God with the mission of his final Prophet. As a distinguished Muslim scholar once said, there can be "no genuine obedience and loyalty to God without obedience and loyalty to His Messenger; nor can there be true acceptance of the testimony that there is no god but Allah without also accepting Muhammad as His messenger."[9] In the Quran, Muhammad himself stresses both his common humanity with all other persons and his unique role as the channel of definitive revelation: "Say: 'I am but a mortal like you; it has been revealed to me that your God is one God'" (18:110). Muslims believe, then, that Muhammad was a human being just like anyone else. At the same time they regard him as unique within the human family because, in the providence of God, he became the vessel through whom God's perfect revelation was given to the Arabs and, through them, to the whole human race. Muhammad was the channel through which the true will of God has been made known in the faith of *Islam*.

Throughout the centuries Christians and Muslims have strongly disagreed about the character and personality of Muhammad. Muslims always speak of Muhammad with great love, respect, and gratitude. They never speak or write his name without adding the acclamation "Peace be upon him." They regard him as the seal of the prophets (33:40), a lamp shining in the darkness (33:46), the perfect exemplar for all human beings (33:21), and a blessing for the whole world (21:107).

Unlike the New Testament, which tells us the story of Jesus, the Quran provides almost no information about Muhammad's life. The first biography of Muhammad was recorded by Muhammad Ibn Ishaq more than one hundred years after the prophet's death. Some modern scholars have undertaken a sort of "quest for the historical Muhammad" because they have found it difficult to disentangle the historical core of his life and work from the many stories and legends that have circulated about him.[10] To cite just a few, it is said that his mother, Aminah, experienced no pain during pregnancy and childbirth, that on one occasion the stones in the streets of Mecca cried out in greeting as he passed near them, that water flowed from between his fingers, and that a wolf once spoke in praise of him. These and other stories about Muhammad were passed on orally and collected in a group of sayings and traditions known as *hadiths*. These sayings cover many aspects of the spiritual life not recorded in the Quran itself. They are held in great respect by devout Muslims. At the same time, there is debate among Muslim scholars as to how literally one should interpret some of these reputed events in the prophet's life.

Even laying aside some of the extreme claims made by later traditions, no Christian can believe what Islam teaches about Muhammad without becoming a Muslim. For example, Muslims interpret Jesus' promise (in John 14:16) to send "another Counselor" to guide the disciples into all truth as a prediction of the coming of Muhammad rather than a prophecy about the Holy Spirit. How could one make such a claim? The Greek word for "Counselor" ("Comforter" or "Helper" in some translations) is *paraclētos*. Muslim scholars suggest, however, that the original word in this text from John's gospel was *periclytos* ("praised one"). This is the Greek translation of the word *Ahmad,* one of the names given to the prophet in the Quran (61:6). There Jesus is quoted as saying, "I am the apostle of Allah to you . . . giving the good news of an apostle who will come after me, his name being Ahmad." There are no variant readings—nor any other evidence—for this supposed corruption of the text in any of the more than 5,000 manuscripts of the Greek New Testament that have survived. However, this example illustrates an important point in the debate between Christians and Muslims over the authority of the Bible.

As we have seen, Muslim theology recognizes Moses, David, and Jesus as authentic prophets of God and precursors of Muhammad. The Pentateuch, the book of Psalms, and the Gospels are also acknowledged as holy books divinely inspired by God. But the trustworthiness of these writings is undermined by the claim that Jewish and Christian scholars have tampered with them, changing their meaning, as the dispute over Jesus' promise in John 14:16 illustrates. On the other hand, the Quran, Muslims say, is God's perfect revelation, which supercedes all the sacred writings that came before it. The Quran itself does not explicitly teach that the previous Scriptures were corrupted and can no longer be trusted. This theory was developed by later Muslim scholars to explain away the irreconcilable differences between the Quran and the Bible. As W. Montgomery Watt, the great scholar of Islam, put it, "The formulation of this doctrine [the so-called corruption of the Bible] is the first important example of what became a normal practice among Muslim scholars, namely, the exaltation of theological dogma above historical fact."[11]

What is at stake in this debate is not merely a tussle over hermeneutics but rather a fundamental cleavage in the understanding of religious authority. Christians cannot accept the claims made on behalf of Muhammad by Islamic theology, but is there a sense in which we can recognize the many true things he did say as a genuine revelation from God? To put the question another way, is it possible to arrive at a more positive assessment of Muhammad than traditional Christian calumnies have allowed?

In the Middle Ages, for example, many people thought that Muhammad was a former cardinal of the church who got mad and started Islam because he was not elected pope. Another vulgar, widely circulated story was that Muhammad had been killed by pigs while he was in the process of urinating. Neither story had any basis in fact, but many Christians repeated and believed

> *There is much in the Quran that is consistent with God's revelation in the Bible.*

these stories for many years.[12] Such stories are no longer repeated by responsible Christian apologists (such as Norman Geisler and Abdul Saleeb, who deal extensively with Muhammad [and how he is perceived by both Christians and Muslims] in their book *Answering Islam: The Crescent in the Light of the Cross*).[13]

Colin Chapman, a British scholar of Islam, has identified four possible responses Christians can make to Muhammad and his message:

1. Some Christians believe that Islam was inspired by the devil and that the angel Gabriel, who is said to have transmitted the Quran to Muhammad, was really a demonic spirit. They believe that Muhammad himself was the incarnation of the antichrist, or the false prophet, whose coming was foretold in the Scriptures. Some even claim that the Quran, like the Book of Mormon, should not be read by true believers, lest their minds be corrupted and led astray by its evil teachings.
2. While not denying that Satan has the ability to masquerade as an angel of light and to foster resistance to the gospel, a second view refuses to single out Islam as a special case of demonic control. The Bible says that the *whole world*, not

just the Islamic world, lies in the power of the evil one (1 John 5:19). Moreover, there is much in the Quran that is consistent with God's revelation in the Bible. We should claim common ground where possible but also help Muslims to understand their need for Jesus and to see the truth that redemption is found only in him.

3. Another perspective points to Muhammad's role in rejecting the polytheism and idolatry of his native Arab culture. The monotheism of Islam is compared to that of the Old Testament, although the nature of God in the Bible is not identical to that of Allah in the Quran. It is also recognized that the covenant blessings given to Israel were fulfilled by Jesus Christ and not reserved for a later installment in the divine economy. One expression of this view states that we should think of Muhammad as being "*chronologically* A.D. but *informationally* B.C."[14]

4. A fourth view regards Muhammad as a genuine prophet for Muslims. It states that he was indeed the messenger of God for the Arab peoples in his day, and that Islam is as equally valid a pathway to God as the Christian pathway revealed in the Bible and in Jesus Christ.[15] Many who hold this view see no reason why Muslims should be persuaded to become followers of Jesus, because Islam provides all they need in order to know and serve God.

How shall we assess these four viewpoints? The first alternative gives the devil too much credit. It ignores the fact that human beings in their fallen, depraved state (whether they live in New York City or Mecca) are fully capable of straying from the straight path—quite apart from special demonic intervention. This view also ignores the fact that God reveals himself in nature, as well as to the consciences of all persons everywhere. As Paul argues in Romans 1 and 2, this general revelation is the basis of our accountability, of our being "without excuse," before God (Romans 1:20). Paul does not teach that this natural knowledge of God issues in a saving relationship with God. But he does say that God "has not left himself without testimony" in every human heart (Acts 14:17; see also Acts 17:27–30). Thus when Muhammad destroyed the man-made idols in Mecca and urged the people there to turn to the one and only creator God, he did something in keeping with biblical faith, even if this act—and the religious system that grew out of it—cannot be considered a part of God's sacred covenant history with his people. But to say this does not mean we must adopt the fourth option above—a perspective that relativizes the truth-claims of both Christianity and Islam. It also undermines the missionary commitment of both religions. Options two and three seem to me more in keeping with both the facts of history and the integrity of the biblical gospel.

Turning Points

Before we leave the story of Muhammad, we would do well to review some of the major events and turning points in his life:

570 – Muhammad was born in the trading city of Mecca. Orphaned at an early age, he was brought up by his uncle, Abu Talib, who took him on trips to Syria and taught him the trade of being a caravan manager. In those days Muhammad was known as *al-Amin,* the "trustworthy one."

595 – Muhammad married Khadijah, a rich widow twenty-five years older than he was. They had several children including a daughter named Fatima. Fatima would later marry Ali, one of the successors (called caliphs) of Muhammad after his death.

610 – During the month of Ramadan in this year, while meditating in a cave on Mount Hira, near Mecca, Muhammad received the first of the revelations that would eventually become the Quran. Muslims believe that the angel Gabriel appeared to Muhammad with a command: "Recite!" (96:1; literally, "make *qur'an*"). These visitations continued intermittently over the next twenty-three years. Muhammad, who could neither read nor write, simply recited to others what he had

been told. These sayings were memorized and written down by others, and in this way the Quran came into being.

619 – A year marked by the death of his uncle and his beloved wife, Khadija, with whom he had shared a monogamous union for twenty-four years. Later he would marry a number of other women, exceeding by divine permission the four wives allotted to a man in the Quran (33:50).

620 – Muhammad's Night Journey (17:1). In this experience Muhammad is said to have been taken by Gabriel to Jerusalem, where the Dome of the Rock now stands. Traveling on his fabulous steed, Buraq, Muhammad ascended, one by one, into the seven heavens, where he met the prophets who had come before him—Moses, Jesus, Abraham, and Adam. As he approached the veil of Divine Unity beyond the seventh heaven, he was granted a vision of God on his throne, an experience of blinding radiance and light. Muslims differ as to whether the Night Journey was a literal event or something more mystical in nature. Muslims commemorate it every year. This helps to explain why Jerusalem is regarded as a holy city by Muslims as well as by Christians and Jews. Some scholars have suggested that Muhammad's Night Journey is comparable to the transfiguration of Jesus. Both events include an experience of divine luminescence and an encounter with prophets of an earlier dispensation.

622 – The year of Muhammad's migration, or flight to Medina. Muhammad's preaching of the one God proved a threat that led to conflict with the leaders of Mecca, who were making great profit from their sponsorship of idol worship. The *Hijra*, or flight to Medina, marked a new beginning for Muhammad and his followers. From that time on, Islam was defined as a political and military (as well as a spiritual) community. Muhammad was not only the prophet but also the ruler and commander-in-chief of his armed forces. Muhammad himself led military campaigns and was once

wounded on the battlefield. Although he suffered some defeats, he experienced a great victory over his enemies at the battle of Badr in 624. On another occasion, he ordered the execution of several hundred Jewish men who had tried to overthrow the Muslim regime in Medina. The year 622 is the birthday of Islam, and all subsequent history is designated A.H. ("After the Hijra").

630 – In this year (8 A.H.), having consolidated his power in Medina, Muhammad marched on Mecca with an army of ten thousand men. The city surrendered, assuring the ascendancy of Islam in Arabia. Muhammad ordered the pagan idols in the *Kabah* to be destroyed. He personally participated in this iconoclastic cleansing by breaking, with his own hands, a pigeon-idol made of wood that was hanging from the roof of the shrine.

632 – Muhammad died and was buried in Medina. The first four caliphs who succeeded him consolidated the power of the Muslim community. They were Abu Bakr (632–34), Umar (634–44), Uthman (644–56), and Ali (656–61). In 732, by the time Charles Martel drove back the Muslim armies at the battle of Poitiers (a city about two hundred miles south of Paris), exactly one century after Muhammad's death, Islam had become a dominant political force in the world. But a debate over Muhammad's successor led to a major split in the Muslim world—a split that continues to this day. Sunni Muslims look back to the period of the first four "rightly guided" caliphs as an Islamic "golden age." On the other hand, Shiites (from *shiat ali*, Ali's Party) regard the first three caliphs as usurpers who should have allowed Ali, Muhammad's cousin and son-in-law, to succeed him in the first place. Other theological, legal, and political divergences have driven these two branches of Islam further apart. Today some 90 percent of the world's Muslims are Sunnis; the Shiites are concentrated mostly in Iran.

CHAPTER TWO

TIES THAT BIND, SCARS THAT HURT

Islam was a perpetual reminder to Christendom of the latter's failure truly to represent her Lord. For if she had done so, Muhammad would have been a Christian.

WILLIAM HENRY TEMPLE GAIRDNER

At the heart of the Christian faith are three fundamental beliefs Islam has always rejected—the Trinity, the Incarnation, and redemption by divine grace through the cross of Jesus Christ. In the following chapters I'll look in detail at these differences. But first, we need to recognize that Christianity and Islam, along with Judaism, do have a number of things in common. In this chapter, I'll investigate five affinities that link Judaism, Christianity, and Islam, albeit with different meanings and divergent emphases even here. Then I'll briefly examine how the Christian witness in the Muslim world has been affected by the long history of mutual antagonisms.

Affinities across the Divide

From one perspective, all religions are about the same thing: the finitude of life, the significance of death, how to find meaning and purpose in a world filled with suffering and pain, and the deep yearnings of the human heart. From the standpoint of biblical revelation, however, the Christian faith cannot be considered as "just another religion." The Bible teaches that God himself has intervened to rescue fallen human beings from sin and folly and to provide what no religion—including a Christianity that is understood as a "religious system"—could ever give, namely, eternal life. Still, in some of its basic assumptions and practices, Christianity bears a striking resemblance to its two Semitic cousins, Judaism and Islam.

Each of these religious communities originated in the Middle East, and each sees itself related in a special way to the patriarch Abraham. They are sometimes called "children of Abraham," as well as "people of the Book." They are all *historical*, or rooted in history. They are all *scriptural*, having sacred texts and holy books they consider divinely inspired. They are all *monotheistic* in that they profess to worship one God, not many. They are all *missionary*, with a worldwide vision to extend their message to all peoples. And they are all *purpose-driven*, believing that history is marching toward a divinely appointed end, a grand finale in which they will play a significant role.

Historical

Jews, Christians, and Muslims affirm in unison that the Almighty Creator of heaven and earth has decisively made known his will in the course of human history. Judaism, Christianity, and Islam are all "historical" religions in that they reject the idea that life is a great wheel ever turning round and round like the cycle of the seasons, year after year. History is the arena of God's activity. He intervenes to direct the course of history toward its predestined end. But each of these traditions has its own special locus or event, a defining moment that gives identity to the community of faith and provides the key to understanding history itself. For Jews this event is the exodus. The exodus not only liberated the Hebrew slaves from bondage in Egypt, but it also led to the giving of the law and the renewal of God's covenant with his people. For Christians, the one decisive event of salvation history is the

Incarnation: "The Word became flesh and made his dwelling among us" (John 1:14). So significant was this event that Christians have marked time by it ever since—B.C. (before Christ) and A.D. (*anno Domini,* "in the year of the Lord").

For Muslims too, God is the Lord of history. He has made known his will through the prophets, some 124,000 in number from Adam to Muhammad. Most of these prophets are unknown, but the Quran mentions twenty-five of them by name. As we have seen, it is the Quran, and not Muhammad himself, that is the unique revelation of God in history that corresponds to the Incarnation in Christianity. Muhammad is merely God's messenger through whom the holy book from heaven was transmitted to earth, just as (for Christians) the Virgin Mary was the vessel through whom God's eternal Word became flesh.

Scriptural

Judaism, Christianity, and Islam are all literate religions. Each possesses a body of holy writings believed to be divinely inspired and normative for the life and faith of the community. For Jews, it is the Torah, which means "divine instruction." For Protestant Christians, it is the thirty-nine books of the Old Testament and the twenty-seven books of the New (Roman Catholics and the Orthodox add several more to the Old Testament). For Muslims, it is the Quran, believed to be the Word of God revealed verbatim to Muhammad over the last several decades of his life. The Quran is about the same size as the New Testament. It contains 114 chapters, called *surahs,* and some 6,000 verses, called *ayat,* a word that literally means "sign." (Thus, an *ayatollah* is a religious leader [among Shiite Muslims] believed to be "the sign of Allah.") The *surahs* are arranged not chronologically but in order of descending length, the longest first and the shortest last. There are eighty-six Meccan *surahs* and twenty-eight *surahs* from the Median period of Muhammad's life. All Muslims believe that the revelation of the Quran was miraculous. How else, they ask, could an illiterate camel-caravan manager transmit inerrantly such a lengthy, complex message from God?

The Quran, like the Jewish Torah and the Christian Bible, has inspired a vast library of exegesis, exposition, and commentary. Only recently have some scholars begun to apply the methods of historical-critical analysis to the text of the Quran. Most Muslims regard this enterprise with disdain and see it as an example of unbelief and spiritual imperialism. When Salman Rushdie published his *Satanic Verses*, a fanciful and irreverent novel about Muhammad and the Quran, he was sentenced to death by Iran's religious leader, Ayatollah Khomeini—though, mercifully for Rushdie, this verdict, or *fatwa*, has not been carried out.

Should we think of a "battle of the books" between the Christian Bible and the Muslim Quran? While there are similarities between the two, there are also crucial differences. The Quran was revealed to just one person over a period of twenty-three years. The Bible was written by scores of individuals in several languages over the course of more than a millenium. From the beginning, Christians have stressed the importance of translating the Bible into every language human beings speak. Special mission groups, such as Wycliffe Bible Translators, have been established for this very purpose. Christians believe that the gospel is culture-permeable. They strive to make the message of Jesus Christ and his love known to all the peoples of the earth in the total context of their life, history, and language. Muslims see the Quran in a very different light: only in the Arabic original is the Quran God's Word. For centuries Muslim scholars refused to translate the Quran at all. Even now, translations of the Quran are regarded as mere interpretations that lack both the spirit and authority of the original.

> *Judaism, Christianity, and Islam share a common passion for the oneness of God.*

Certain Christian groups have made similar claims about specific versions of the Bible, too. For many years, Roman Catholics held to the special status of the Bible in Latin. Some conservative Protestants still say that only the King James Version has divine authority. But these are distortions of the Christian understanding of Holy Scripture. While the Bible was inspired in the privileged languages of revelation—Greek, Hebrew, and Aramaic—it is intended for "every tribe and language and people and nation" on earth (Revelation 5:9).

Monotheistic

Judaism, Christianity, and Islam share a common passion for the oneness of God, the transcendent Creator and Lord of all that is. The flight from idolatry is inherent in the "no other gods before me" of the Ten Commandments, as well as the "no god but God" of the *Shahada*. Shunning idols is also a major theme in the New Testament. Paul describes the process of conversion to Jesus as a turning from idols to serve the true and living God (1 Thessalonians 1:9). John ends his first epistle with an urgent command: "Dear children, keep yourselves from idols" (1 John 5:21).

For monotheistic religions, idolatry must be shunned at all costs, because the one God—the only real God—demands undivided loyalty. This is the source of the exclusive claims, so offensive to modern ears, made by each of these Abrahamic traditions. As the psalmist says of God, "He has revealed his word to Jacob, his laws and decrees to Israel. *He has done this for no other nation*" (Psalm 147:19–20, emphasis added). Christians believe that Jesus Christ is not only the unique Son of God and sole Savior of the world but also the coming Judge and King of all. While Islam could never accept such a claim for Muhammad, it does regard him as God's final prophet, the chief messenger through whom the one true and definitive way to God has been revealed for all time.

Some scholars have argued that monotheism is inherently racist, oppressive, and violent—witness the many holy wars waged in the name of the one true God. But it could just as well be argued that these tendencies, though real enough historically, represent a de facto denial of true monotheism. In other words, when we elevate a particular race, tribe, or ideology to the place that rightly belongs to God alone, we slide back into a kind of practical polytheism—the worship of Blood and Soil, Black or White, Left or Right. Destructiveness and evil in human life do not issue from commitment to the one true God; they signal a return of the idols.

Missionary

With its ethnic particularism and lack of aggressive evangelism, Judaism might not seem to fit this theme. But the missionary character of Israel's vocation is unmistakable from the Hebrew Scriptures. God wanted Abraham and his descendants to be "a light for the Gentiles" (Isaiah 49:6), and the prophets again and again called them back to this mission. The Law was given to Israel not as their private possession but in order that they might live it out "in the sight of the nations" (Deuteronomy 4:6 KJV) and thus others would also come to recognize the awesome glory of God. The missionary impulse in Christianity derives not only from Jesus' command to "go and make disciples of all nations" (Matthew 28:19) but also from the pattern of his own life and ministry. By reaching out in love and grace to all sorts of people—Samaritan women, Roman centurions, Greek intellectuals, and the like—Jesus demonstrated that his message was meant for all persons everywhere. When the early church decided to include Gentiles along with Jews among Jesus-followers, this decision had far-reaching implications. Christianity thus emerged as a universal religion, comprising many different races, cultures, and language groups.

Islam shares with Judaism and Christianity a world-embracing missionary mentality. When Muhammad reconstituted the Muslim community in Medina after the *Hijra,* he made belief in Allah, not ties of tribe and family, the basis for participation in the *ummah*. This new inclusivism undoubtedly contributed to the amazing spread of Islam from the Pyrenees to the Himalayas; Muslim traders, no less than Muslim soldiers, both carried the message of Muhammad throughout the Mediterranean, African, and Asian worlds.

Because of widespread prejudice and persecution against the Jews in the Middle Ages, the missionary motif in Judaism was largely sublimated into the instinct for survival, leaving Christianity and Islam the two vital competitors in the evangelization of the world. But their evangels were radically different—and both Christians and Muslims ended up calling one another "infidels." Sadly, the rivalry turned violent.

Purpose-Driven

Because of their belief in the Creator-God who made the world and acts in its history, the three great Semitic religions are each teleological, from the Greek *telos,* which means "purpose," or "goal." For all three monotheistic religions, the God of creation and history is also the God of final judgment. The "Day of the Lord" is a major theme in the Old Testament prophets. Ezekiel, Daniel, and Zechariah described the final climactic end of history in vivid apocalyptic imagery. In the New Testament, the second coming of Jesus, called the *parousia,* is described in similar ways, not only in the book of Revelation, but in many of Paul's writings and in the Gospels as well. Islam also teaches that the world as we know it now will come to an end in a great cosmic upheaval (81:1–14) marked by the return of Jesus in glory, the defeat of the antichrist, the bodily resurrection of all who have died, and the final meting out of rewards and punishments before the bar of Allah's judgment.

> *The God of creation and history is also the God of final judgment.*

Like John the Baptist and Jesus in the New Testament, Muhammad brought a message of imminent judgment. According to one tradition, he once held up his thumb and forefinger and pointed to the tiny space between them. "I and the last hour are like this," he said.[1] It was this kind of preaching that got him in trouble with the merchants of Mecca. They resented his preaching about a day of resurrection and reckoning: "What! When we are dead and turned to dust and bones, shall we be raised to life, we and our forefathers?" they asked indignantly (37:16–17). Judaism, Christianity, and Islam are all profoundly otherworldly religions. Heaven and hell are more real than the life we know here and now, and this present world is a "getting-ready place" for a more permanent abode.

Does this firm belief in eschatology make one passive and resigned in this present world? Not at all. Awareness of a rendezvous with God in eternity gives urgency to life here and now. As the New Testament puts it, "Since everything will be destroyed in this way, what kind of people ought you to be?" (2 Peter 3:11). All three religions have had their mystics and pietists who stressed the inwardness of faith, but in their mainstream orthodox expressions, they have all been activist, culture-shaping traditions committed to the historical unfolding of God's divine purpose and will.

Crusades for Christ?

Theology can never be carried out in a vacuum. In a book that seeks to understand some of the major doctrinal differences between Christianity and Islam, it's impossible to ignore 1400 years of a conflicted history. It is a story more often written in blood than with ink. Dwight D. Eisenhower described the Allied effort to defeat the Nazis in World War II as a "Crusade" in Europe. After the war, many evangelical ministries began to use this same word to describe their efforts to share the message of Jesus with others. Most of us are familiar with Campus Crusade for Christ, the Billy Graham Crusades, Christian Literature Crusade, and so forth. But the word *crusade* has fallen on hard times of late. Wheaton College (Wheaton, Illinois) recently changed the name of its athletic teams from the Crusaders to the more generic Thunder, reflecting the liability of a label associated in the popular mind with medieval holy wars.

No one who has lived or traveled in the Middle East can be unaware of the lingering resentment felt toward the "Latins," as the Crusaders are called. This bitterness extends beyond Muslims to Greek Orthodox Christians, who have never forgotten the trauma of the Fourth Crusade of 1204. On that occasion, Crusaders from the West, marching under the banner of the cross, raped and pillaged Constantinople, doing to their fellow Christians what no Muslim army had been able to do up to that point. Missiology expert Ruth Tucker has written of the lingering effect of the Crusading mentality on Christian missions: "So bitter was the animosity of Muslims towards Christians, as a result of the savage cruelty manifested during the Crusades, that even today the memory has not been erased, and evangelism remains most difficult among people of the Muslim faith."[2]

But seen from another perspective, the Crusades were but a delayed reaction to earlier Muslim aggression. Beginning with the fall of Jerusalem in 636, Muslim armies captured, blitzkrieg-like, all of the major urban centers of early Christianity—Antioch, Damascus, Alexandria, and Carthage (the city of Tertullian, Cyprian, and Augustine). In 1453 Constantinople itself fell to the Ottoman Turks, the ruling force in the Muslim world at that time. During the Reformation, the armies of Islam in the 1520s were pressing on the gates of Vienna. They continued to do so periodically until they were finally turned back in 1683. Leaders of the Christian West were not being paranoid when they saw their civilization threatened by militant Islam.

The Crusades were a violent, sporadic, and ultimately ineffectual response to this threat. When Pope Urban II called for an international counter-jihad to liberate the Holy Land from the infidels, thousands of people responded *deus vult* ("God wills it"). Bernard of Clairvaux, among others, encouraged the Knights of Europe to do the honorable thing by taking up the sword under the banner of the cross:

> Our King [Jesus] is accused of treachery; it is said of him [by the Muslims] that he is not God, but that he falsely pretended to be something he was not. Any man among you who is his vassal ought to rise up to defend his Lord from the infamous accusation of treachery; he should go to the sure fight, where to win will be glorious and where to die will be gain.[3]

In 1099 Jerusalem fell to the Crusaders. They slaughtered all Muslims and Jews, including women and children. They converted the Dome of the Rock into a church. This victory was short-lived, however, as the famous general Saladin recaptured the Holy City in 1187. In 1291 the final Crusader forces were defeated at Acre, and Christians were expelled from the Holy Land. From then on until the end of World War I, the holy sites of Jerusalem were under the control of Muslim forces.

At the conclusion of his magisterial three-volume study of the Crusades, Steven Runciman offered this assessment:

> In the long sequence of interaction and fusion between Orient and Occident out of which our civilization has grown, the Crusades were a tragic and destructive episode. The historian as he gazes back across the centuries at their gallant story must find his admiration overcast by sorrow at the witness that it bears to the limitations of human nature. There is so much courage and so little honor, so much devotion and so little understanding. High ideals were besmirched by cruelty and greed, enterprise and endurance by blind and narrow self-righteousness.[4]

The bitter historical interaction of Christians and Muslims, from the era of the Crusades onward, colors our discussions about the meaning of *jihad* in Islam today. The word *jihad* comes from the verb *jahada,* which means "to exert oneself." To practice *jihad* means to use all one's strength, might, and soul in the service of Allah, "striving or struggling in the way of God."

According to a non-Quranic tradition, Muhammad once returned from battle and declared, "We have returned from the lesser *jihad* to the greater *jihad.*" "What is the greater *jihad*?" he was asked. "It is the struggle against oneself," he replied. There are passages in the Quran that support the idea of Islam as a religion not given to violence and war, such as "God guides such as follow his pleasure into the ways of peace, and brings them out of darkness into light by his will, and guides them to the right path" (5:16) and the oft-quoted "Let there be no compulsion in religion" (2:256).

Yet, in the spirit of the quotation from Bernard of Clairvaux cited above, many other texts clearly sanction armed conflict against unbelievers in the name of God: "Make war on them until idolatry shall cease and God's religion shall reign supreme" (8:39; see also 4:89; 4:76; 8:60; 9:5). Trying to sort out the meaning of these and other texts is like trying to watch a theological Ping-Pong match! Fundamentally, this is not a dispute between Christianity and Islam but rather a debate within Islam itself. The lesser *jihad* / greater *jihad* distinction was given classic exposition by the great medieval scholar al Ghazali and has been quoted with favor by more moderate Muslims in recent times. These are the people who say that the religion of Islam has been hijacked by the likes of Osama bin Laden and his fellow terrorists.

It would be a mistake, however, to write off Islamism—the name scholars give to recent militant radicalism in Islam—as the work of a few extremist crackpots. No, this perspective (and the various action plans it has engendered) reflects deeply rooted impulses in the Muslim world. These include a negative reaction to "Western" culture (with its traditions of human rights and religious freedom), the forceful imposition of harsh Islamic law in Muslim countries (including, in some places, the brutal oppression of women), and a willingness to engage in, or at least to approve of, violent acts of assassination and terrorism in the name of Allah. Islamists refer to more moderate Muslims who lack sympathy for their revolutionary activities as renegades and traitors to the true faith of Muhammad. They, not the appeasing moderates, they say, are the true interpreters of *jihad*—the holy warriors who do battle with the infidels and the enemies of Islam.

Perhaps more important than the precise meaning of *jihad* is whether Islam as a culture, or civilization, can develop an understanding of the state that can religiously legitimize genuine diversity, freedom of religion, and the right to dissent. It shouldn't surprise us that Muslims are reluctant to embrace the democratic models of the West, given the inroads of secularism in and the expulsion of spiritual values from much of our public life. And yet, Richard John Neuhaus offers this wise assessment:

51

From the beginning, Christianity has had the great asset of what some derisively call its "dualism"—the conceptual resource for distinguishing between spiritual and temporal authority, which has given it enormous flexibility in relating to different political and cultural circumstances from Theodosius to Hildebrand to the religion clause of the U.S. Constitution. Islam is emphatically monistic. This is a great asset when joined to military and political power in the course of conquest, but a disabling weakness under the conditions of postmodernity.[5]

A More Excellent Way

In the early years of the Reformation, when it seemed that Europe might be run over by the Muslim armies of the Ottoman Turks, there was much talk about recruiting soldiers for a new Crusade. Although he was no pacifist, Martin Luther was opposed to this idea. The church should not fight with a sword, he said. There are other weapons it must wield, another kind of warfare it should wage, and thus it "must not mix itself up with the wars of the emperor and the princes." What if we sent evangelists rather than warriors to the Turks? he asked. Perhaps some of the Muslims there would be converted "when they see that Christians surpass the Turks in humility, patience, diligence, fidelity, and such like virtues."[6]

As far as we know, Luther's ideal missionary to the Muslims never made it to Istanbul. But earlier in the Middle Ages, at the height of the Crusades, Francis of Assisi did undertake a famous mission to the Muslim sultan Melek-al-Kamil, personally embodying an alternative engagement with the Muslim world. Later, in his *Rule of 1221*, Francis set forth regulations for his disciples who desired to become missionaries. They should be prepared, he said, "to expose themselves to every enemy, visible and invisible, for love of Christ."[7]

In 1900 there were 200 million Muslims in the world. Samuel Zwemer, the great scholar-missionary, estimated that since five out of six Muslims at that time were in countries under British rule, it would only be a matter of time before almost all would become Christians. Zwemer set forth his ideas in a book titled *The Disintegration of Islam.* Now, a century later, we know only too well what Zwemer could not have known: the dissolution of the British Empire, the impact of the rise and fall of Communism on the Islamic world, the creation of independent Muslim nation-states, the emergence of Islamic fundamentalism, and the loss of a missionary vision on the part of many Christians in the West. But Zwemer, like William Carey and Henry Martyn

> *What if we sent evangelists rather than warriors?*

before him, had a resolute faith in the sovereignty of God. The success of Christ's kingdom cannot be measured in what educators like to call "outcomes assessment." William Carey preached seven years in India before baptizing his first convert from Hinduism. Henry Martyn was buried in a lonely grave in Turkey, having "burned out" for God at the age of thirty-one.

In recent years, a new awareness of the Muslim world has emerged among evangelical Christians. We have been called to pray for our brothers and sisters in Christ who live in Muslim lands—many of whom face persecution, duress, and even death because they are Jesus-followers. We've also learned much about Muslim culture and the importance of building bridges to Islam for the sake of the gospel from the writings and work of Kenneth Cragg, Colin Chapman, Phil Parshall, Miriam Adeney, Norman Anderson, George Braswell, Bill Musk, Ron George, and others. Even assuming the best of motives, which was not always evident, the Crusaders missed the mark. Francis, not Richard the Lionheart, got it right. In Jesus' name, we still reach out under the banner of the cross but with a different objective—not to retake from Islam what Christendom has lost, as the Crusades tried to do, but to share with Muslims the Christ they have missed.[8]

CHAPTER THREE

IS THE FATHER OF JESUS THE GOD OF MUHAMMAD?

Christians and Muslims alike passionately proclaim belief in one God. But everything depends on the meaning we put into the word "God."

STEPHEN NEILL

Among the many distinctive truths Christians proclaim, the one that sets them apart from Islam most fundamentally is this: The God of the Bible is the God who has forever known himself, and who in Jesus Christ has revealed himself to us, as *the Father, the Son, and the Holy Spirit*. This is the doctrine of the Holy Trinity. The Trinity is the basis for the entire Christian life—the basis of everything we believe and teach. And it is something confessed by all orthodox Christians—Greek Orthodox Christians, Roman Catholic Christians, historic Protestant Christians, and others as well.

Ironically, the doctrine of the Trinity may be at one and the same time the most important and the most neglected doctrine we hold. We are baptized in the name of the Father and the Son and the Holy Spirit. We often hear that wonderful Pauline benediction, "May the grace of the Lord Jesus Christ, and the love of

God, and the fellowship of the Holy Spirit be with you all" (2 Corinthians 13:14). Yet we so often neglect this teaching.

Why? Perhaps because we cannot understand or explain the Trinity. How can one plus one plus one equal one *and* three at the same time? Isn't this mathematical madness? Someone has said that those who deny the doctrine of the Trinity may lose their souls, whereas those who try to explain it will certainly lose their minds! Doesn't the Bible warn against pursuing "foolish and stupid arguments" that breed quarrels (2 Timothy 2:23)? What could be more sterile and useless than a dispute over how to reconcile unity and plurality in the being of God? Is the Trinity even mentioned in the Four Spiritual Laws? No wonder many Christians, evangelicals no less than those with more liberal bents, are happy to follow the lead of Friedrich Schleiermacher, who relegated the doctrine of the Trinity to a few lines at the end of his massive systematic theology titled *The Christian Faith*. The less said the better!

> *The Trinity is the basis for the entire Christian life.*

But belief in the Trinity cannot be so easily cast aside in the Christian encounter with Islam. To Muslims, the Christian belief in God as One and Three seems not only inherently contradictory but also inexcusably derogatory—a denial of the unity of God, for which the harsh word *kufr* (deliberate truth-concealing, and lying about God) is not too severe. I believe that we Christians need to revisit the doctrine of the Trinity, not only for apologetic purposes, but also to rekindle our love and devotion to the one true God, the God who in Christ was reconciling the world to himself (2 Corinthians 5:18). In this chapter, after looking first at some statements about the Trinity in the Quran, I want to show how the Trinitarian faith is rooted in biblical revelation. Then, in the following chapter, I aim to extend the discussion further by asking what is so decisively at stake in the Christian understanding of the triune God.

Muslim Misperceptions?

There are several places in the Quran where the Trinity seems to be explicitly denied:

- Unbelievers are those who say: "God is one of three." There is but one God. If they do not desist from so saying, those of them that disbelieve shall be sternly punished (5:73).
- Then God will say: "Jesus son of Mary, did you ever say to mankind: 'Worship me and my mother as gods besides God?' " "Glory be to you," he will answer, "I could never have claimed what I have no right to.... I told them only what you bade me. I said: 'Serve God, my Lord and your Lord' " (5:114).
- People of the Book, do not transgress the bounds of your religion. Speak nothing but the truth about God. Believe in God and his apostles and do not say: "Three": ... God will not forgive idolatry. He that serves other gods besides God has strayed far indeed (4:171, 114).

These verses are often cited in Muslim polemics against the Christian doctrine of the Trinity. But some scholars have questioned whether this is really a valid interpretation. The question is this: Do these verses oppose a truly *Christian* concept of God, or do they misconstrue the latter for what is really a heretical caricature of this teaching?

To answer this question we have to go back to the world into which Muhammad was born and in which he grew up. His grandfather had been the curator of the *Kabah* in Mecca. Today this cubelike block structure is the focal point for Muslim worship, and we often see it portrayed in media stories about Islam. Before Muhammad, however, this famous shrine was the center of polytheistic worship in Arabia. Camel caravans and Bedouin tribes from the desert went there to offer sacrifices and pay homage to the sacred objects and local deities. The *Kabah* was a veritable pantheon of such deities—360 in all, one for nearly every day of the year. We know the names of some of these gods. Three of them—Allat, Al-Uzza, and Manat—were acclaimed by the pagans of Mecca to be the "daughters of Allah" (53:19–20). The idea that the Almighty God of Creation should cohabit with mortals and produce progeny was anathema to Muhammad. "What! Shall you have sons, and Allah daughters?" he asked in derision (53:21). It was the mission of Muhammad to destroy this kind of idolatry root and branch.

It is important to remember that Muhammad was born less than two centuries after Saint Augustine died. The doctrine of the Trinity had been clarified and defined by Christians only after centuries of controversy and debate within the church. The Council of Nicaea in A.D. 325 declared that the Son was of the same essence as the Father. This countered the view of Arius, a presbyter in Alexandria, who believed that the Son had been created by the Father. The meaning of this teaching was further clarified at three other important church councils—at Constantinople in 381, at Ephesus in 431, and finally at Chalcedon in 451 where the incarnate Christ was declared to be one person (the second person of the Holy Trinity) in two natures: the one nature fully human and the other nature fully divine.

> *The Bible is thoroughly Trinitarian from first to last.*

These were—and are—complex notions. It is not surprising that, given the ferocity of the debates and the issues at stake, many Christians did not "get it" all at once. Tritheism, which makes a trio out of the Trinity, continued to flourish on the margins of Christianity for several centuries. This heretical view sometimes appeared in a sophisticated philosophical form—such as that of John Philoponus. More often, however, tritheism flourished in the more crass and literal versions of popular piety.

Apparently Muhammad had encountered certain quasi-Christians of this latter sort who taught something like this: God the Father had sexual intercourse with the Virgin Mary, resulting in the conception of Jesus. Where did such a bizarre idea come from? The early church father, Epiphanius, tells of a fourth-century heretical sect called the Collyridians. Made up mostly of women, they regarded the Virgin Mary as a goddess and sacrificed little round cakes to her called *collyris*. We have no evidence that Muhammad came into contact with this particular group, but it is not hard to see how an exaggerated devotion to Mary, together with Eastern portrayals of the Madonna and Child, might have reinforced Muslim misperceptions of the Christian doctrine of the Trinity.[1]

We do know that Muhammad had contact with more orthodox Christian believers later in his life. We also know that one of the wives he married after Khadija's death was a Coptic Christian from Egypt. However, what is rejected in the Quran itself is not the proper Christian doctrine of the Trinity but rather a heretical belief in three gods. Christians believe just as strongly as Muslims in the *oneness* of God. We can only agree with the Quran in its rejection of a concocted tritheism.

Christian Affirmations

The word *Trinity* is not found in the Bible, but the Bible itself is thoroughly Trinitarian from first to last. Despite the fact that Islam regards the Bible as corrupted and unreliable, the Quran itself encourages Muslims to read the Law, the Psalms, and the Gospel—as these Scriptures are called. It is thus imperative for Christians to understand the biblical basis of the Trinitarian doctrine of God. In simplest terms, we can say this: *The doctrine of the Trinity is the necessary theological framework for understanding the story of Jesus as the story of God.* It is the exposition of the Old Testament affirmation "God is one" and the New Testament confession "Jesus is Lord," neither of which can be understood apart from the person of the Holy Spirit.

God Is One: *the Unity of God*

We begin with a confession that *God is one*. Christians are just as vehement as Jews and Muslims in affirming what is known in

Islam as *tawhid*—a loyal recognition of the fundamental unity of God, a sentiment enshrined in the first formula of the *Shahada*: "There is no god but God." This confession goes back to Deuteronomy 6:4 (the famous *Shema Israel*): "Hear, O Israel: the LORD our God, the LORD is one." This thought is repeated throughout the Old Testament. Jesus quotes this statement in the New Testament as the first and greatest of all the commandments: "Hear, O Israel, the Lord our God, the Lord is one. Love the Lord your God with all your heart and with all your soul and with all your mind and with all your strength" (Mark 12:29–39). Jesus believed and taught the oneness of God as foundational to his own messianic vocation.

How did this belief in the oneness of God arise within the faith of Israel? It was the cornerstone of God's self-revelation to Moses and the prophets over against the polytheism of the culture around them. Like Arabia in the time of Muhammad, the ancient world of the Jews was filled with numerous competing deities. It was a world in which nature—animals, trees, rivers—was regarded as divine, or at least under the control of various divinities. Out of this setting arose the tradition of idolatry, against which the Old Testament prophets blasted again and again with furious power.

Polytheism is the religion of paganism. The Hebrew prophets attacked it as vigorously, and sometimes as violently, as Muhammad did. Why? Because they saw in the worship of the idols a relapse into the world of unreality. This is why Jeremiah scorns the idols of wood and silver made by the craftsmen who painted and covered them in blue and purple clothes—all dressed up but nowhere to go! They are "senseless and foolish," "worthless," "a fraud," "objects of mockery"; they cannot speak or walk but must be carried everywhere, like the dummies they really are, like "a scarecrow in a melon patch" (Jeremiah 10:1–16).

By contrast, the God who created heaven and earth is the living God, the eternal King, the Maker of all things. He alone is worthy of worship and praise: "This is what the LORD says—Israel's King and Redeemer, the LORD Almighty: I am the first and I am the last; apart from me there is no God" (Isaiah 44:6). This same message was preached without compromise in the New Testament by Jesus, the apostles, and the evangelists. In speaking to the worshipers of Zeus and Hermes in Lystra, Paul and Barnabas declared, "We are bringing you good news, telling you to turn from these worthless things to the living God, who made heaven and earth and sea and everything in them" (Acts 14:15; see also Acts 17:29–30).

In the Bible, the nature and character of God is not arrived at by philosophical speculation but by looking at the words and acts of God in history. Nothing is more clear in the Old Testament than the fundamental oneness of God. Yet in the context of such an unyielding monotheism, we can recognize foreshadowings of the Trinitarian revelation in the Old Testament. It is there at the creation. In the beginning, God created by speaking his word, and the Spirit of God (the *ruach*) was also there—hovering over the darkness that was over the surface of the deep. There are the "divine plurals" of Genesis 1:26 ("Let us make man in our own image") and Isaiah 6:8 ("Who will go for us?"). There is the angel of the Lord, who wrestles with Jacob at the river Jabbok, leaving Jacob—blessed but broken—to say, "I saw God face to face" (Genesis 32:30).

All of this points to a living, dynamic, nonstatic oneness—to a God who is characterized by self-distinction, *a God who can communicate himself* as well as his will to human beings made in his image. When Christians in the early church read these Old Testament passages in the light of Jesus Christ, they saw there vestiges of the Trinity. But the Trinity was not spelled out in clarity and fullness all at once. It took time in God's unfolding revelation to achieve that clarity. Not until Jesus Christ himself came "when the time had fully come," as Paul puts it in Galatians 4:4, were God's children able to see through the veil and behold in the face of Jesus "the light of the knowledge of the glory of God" (2 Corinthians 4:6).

There are many other foreshadowings in the Old Testament as well. For example, in Proverbs, wisdom is frequently spoken of, and sometimes treated as, a personification of God himself. By wisdom God created all things (Proverbs 3:19). In the New Testament, we find wisdom spoken of in the closest association with Jesus Christ, almost as though it were one of his proper names (see 1 Corinthians 1:30; 2:7–8). Then there are all the amazing theophanies and Christophanies (visible manifestations of God or Christ)—the three mysterious visitors that came to see Abraham (Genesis 18:2), the fourth man Nebuchadnezzar saw walking in the flames of the fiery furnace (Daniel 3:24–25)—events pointing beyond themselves to a fuller revelation yet to come. Saint Augustine expressed this principle well in a wonderful Latin phrase: *in vetere testamento novum latet et in novo vetus patet* ("In the old covenant the new is concealed, as in the new the old is revealed"[2]).

Jesus Is Lord: the Deity of Christ

The unity of God revealed in the Old Testament—and reiterated and reconfirmed in the New—is given a fuller, deeper exposition in the light of Jesus' life and ministry. The Old Testament affirmation "God is one" is matched by the New Testament confession "Jesus is Lord." To call Jesus Lord, not just with the lips but from the heart, is to become a Christian, for it is also to recognize Almighty God as heavenly Father, and this can only happen through the power of the Holy Spirit (Galatians 4:6; 1 Corinthians 12:3). To say "Jesus is Lord" is the New Testament way of declaring the deity of Jesus Christ—of affirming his essential oneness with the Father.

This theme is woven throughout the entire New Testament, but nowhere is it more explicitly developed than in the prologue to John's gospel (John 1:1–18). It is not a coincidence that two key books of the Bible begin with the same phrase:

- Genesis 1:1—"In the beginning God created. . . ." God spoke, and worlds that were not came into being.
- John 1:1: "In the beginning was the Word, and the Word was with God, and the Word was God. He was with God in the beginning."

What "beginning" does John refer to? It is a beginning that antedates the Incarnation. It goes beyond and even before the creation. It is a beginning before all other beginnings. The Greek is simple: *en archē,* as the primordial first principle of all things and all times—in the beginning that we can speak of only as eternity. In this beginning was the Word, and the Word was with God, and the Word was God.

John is speaking about what we must call a relationship. The Word was "with God" (Greek, *pros ton theon*), which really means, "face to face with God." In the verse that concludes John's prologue (1:18), we read, "No one has ever seen God, but God, the One and Only, who is at the Father's side, has made him known." Regrettably, this rendering in the NIV doesn't

> *Jesus Christ has shared with the Father an eternal life of intimacy.*

capture the depth of meaning in the relationship between the Father and the Word. The King James Version gets closer to the sense of the text when it declares that Jesus was "in the bosom of the Father."

"At the Father's side"? You can go to a ball game with someone who walks alongside you. That's a chum, a friend. This is *not* the concept John wants to get across. No, the Word, the one who was "in the beginning face to face" with God, is the very one "which is in the bosom of the Father"—this connotes an intimacy, a relationship, a unity that a mere "alongside" comes nowhere near. John is saying that Jesus Christ, the one who has come to make God known to us, has shared with the Father an eternal life of intimacy and intercommunion, a life of mutual self-giving and love "in the bosom" of the Father from all eternity.

One verse in John's prologue summarizes the Christian faith more completely than any other text in the Bible: "And the Word was made flesh, and dwelt among us, (and we beheld his glory, the glory as of the only begotten of the Father,) full of grace and truth" (1:14 KJV). Some translations read, "And the Word became a human being." But the meaning goes deeper and is stronger than that. The Word became *flesh*. Flesh is the part of our human reality that is most vulnerable, gets sick, grows tired, and experiences disease, decay, and death. This is the stupendous claim the Bible makes. *Allah* (the Arabic name for God) *became flesh . . . God was in Christ.*

This was, and is, a scandalous thought, not only to orthodox Muslims, but also to Jewish teachers, Greek philosophers, and religious thinkers of all kinds. Christianity stands or falls with the Incarnation, just as it stands or falls with the Trinity. The glory of the Trinity is that God was able to share his life with the world he had made—and to do so without ceasing to be truly God, without compromising his fundamental unity. The wonder of the Incarnation is not only that God *could* do this, but that he was *willing* to do this. The wonder is that, in fact, in fleshly fact, he has actually *done* so.

How was the reality of God recognized in the ministry of Jesus? Not so much by divine assertion as by inference and implication from his words and deeds. These five activities, among others, set Jesus apart from all other prophets and rabbis who came before or after him:

1. Jesus' remarkable freedom to teach with authority and to fulfill the law and reinterpret it according to a higher standard, as seen, for example, in his "but I tell you" sayings (Matthew 5:17–48)
2. Jesus' ability to drive out demons and confront Satan (Matthew 11:14–22)
3. Jesus' unique filial relationship with God (Matthew 11:27)
4. Jesus' bestowal of unconditional forgiveness (Mark 2:1–12; Luke 15:11–32)
5. Jesus' receiving of worship from others, including the acclamation of Thomas after the resurrection ("My Lord and my God!" [John 20:28])

As the early church reflected on these and other events in Jesus' life, they realized that they were in touch with a reality and a power that could only be accounted for as the presence of God himself in their midst. And so they remembered one of the names associated with his nativity ("Immanuel—which means, 'God with us'" [Matthew 1:23]).

The Holy Spirit as Personal Reality

These first two Christian affirmations—God is one, and Jesus is Lord—have been doubted and denied and fought over by Christian theologians from New Testament times onward. In the second century, the unity of God was called into question by a heretic named Marcion. He was excommunicated from the church at Rome in A.D. 144. Marcion said, in effect, "I like the God of Jesus. He's a God of love; he's a God of mercy and tenderness. But I don't like the God of the Old Testament. He's a mean God, a mad God, a God of war and violence." So Marcion proposed that the entire Old Testament be cut out of the Bible. But the church said, No, *we're not going down that road*. It was perhaps the single most important decision made in the history of Christian doctrine. The dualism of Marcion would have torn apart the essential unity of God. By declaring that the Father of Jesus is the God of Israel— the God of the Old Testament—the church affirmed a fundamental connection between creation and redemption. More than anything else, this decision saved Christianity from becoming just another mystery religion, simply a private salvation-cult unconcerned with the real world of space, time, and history.

The lordship and deity of Jesus Christ was denied in the fourth century by a man named Arius. His theology was a catalyst for the formulation of the doctrine of the Trinity at the Council of Nicaea, and I'll return to his ideas in the next chapter. When Arius denied that the Son of God was of the same fundamental reality as the Father, the church had to say, No, *we can't and won't go that way either*. The one whom we adore and worship and love—Jesus our Redeemer—is *of the same essence* as the Father. We are not talking about two different gods. We are talking about only *one* God, but this one God has forever known himself as the Father, the Son, and the Holy Spirit. Edward

Cooper puts it this way in his 1805 hymn "Father in Heaven, Whose Love Profound":

> Jehovah—Father, Spirit, Son—
> Mysterious Godhead, Three in One,
> Before Thy throne we sinners bend;
> Grace, pardon, life to us extend.

The third central Christian affirmation is that the Holy Spirit is personal. There was a long and bitter struggle over this claim as well. Many thought of the Holy Spirit as a force, an energy, a power—but *not* God. Over against the Spirit-fighters (called this because they challenged the deity of the Holy Spirit), the church declared that God is *one in essence* and *three in person*. The Holy Spirit, no less than the Father and the Son, is fully divine. In the New Testament, the Holy Spirit baptizes (1 Corinthians 12:13); he can be grieved (Ephesians 4:30); he groans (Romans 8:26). These are all things *a person* does. The Holy Spirit is a person and in relation to the Father and the Son—yet one God, forever and ever.

Great Is the Mystery

The difference between Christianity and Islam over the doctrine of the Trinity is not a question about the oneness of God. It is a question about the *nature* of that oneness. Both faith traditions affirm without hesitation the absolute uniqueness and unity of the one God over against all idolatry and polytheism. But Christians believe that the unity of God can allow differentiation without fragmentation. It remains for us to say why this teaching is so important, why, in fact, it is at the heart of the Christian faith. Beyond all question, Paul says, great is the mystery of our faith (1 Timothy 3:16). At the end of the day, we have to admit that the Trinity remains, ultimately, a mystery. Even in eternity we will never comprehend it. But we are called to confess it and believe it and live out our lives in the light of the one God who is merciful and mighty—and perfect in power, in love, and in purity. We confess the Holy Trinity with godly humility and awe, the kind of trembling response John experienced on the island of Patmos as he fell at the feet of the risen Christ. In the revelation of the Trinity, God invites us into the innermost sanctuary of his own eternal heart. And we can only respond with surprise and wonder at such grace.

We confess the Holy Trinity with godly humility and awe.

The Trinity leads to humility, and it issues forth in doxology. Sadly, hymns about the Trinity are seldom sung anymore, except for Reginald Heber's majestic "Holy, Holy, Holy! Lord God Almighty!" But there is a wonderful hymn by the Latin poet Prudentius, who lived in the fourth century when the struggle for the doctrine of the Trinity was still a matter of life and death in the church. Prudentius's "Of the Father's Love Begotten" invites us to join our praise with that of the angels and the saints above:

Christ, to Thee with God the Father
And, O Holy Ghost, to Thee,
Hymn and chant and high thanksgiving
And unwearied praises be.
Honor, glory, and dominion,
And eternal victory,
Evermore and evermore! Amen.

CHAPTER FOUR

WHY THE TRINITY MATTERS

A Christian who unreservedly believes in the Trinity is closer to the Islamic concept of God than a Christian who dilutes the notion of the Trinity for the sake of a unitarianism that quickly flounders into humanism.

SEYYED HOSSEIN NASR

Is the Father of Jesus the God of Muhammad? The answer to this question is surely both yes and no. Yes, in the sense that the Father of Jesus is the only God there is. He is the sovereign Creator and Judge of Muhammad, Confucius, Buddha—indeed, of every person who has ever lived, except Jesus, the one through whom God made the world and will one day judge it (Acts 17:31; Colossians 1:16). The Father of Jesus is the one before whom all shall one day bow the head and bend the knee (Philippians 2:5–11). It is also true that Christians and Muslims can together affirm many important truths about this great God—his oneness, eternity, power, majesty. As the Quran puts it, God is "the Living, the Everlasting, the All-High, the All-Glorious" (2:256).

But the answer to the question "Is the Father of Jesus the God of Muhammad?" is also no, for Muslim theology rejects the fatherhood of God, the deity of Jesus Christ, and the personhood of the

Holy Spirit—each of which is an essential component of the Christian understanding of God. No devout Muslim can call the God of Muhammad "father," for this, in Islamic thought, would compromise divine transcendence. But no faithful Christian can refuse to confess with joy and confidence, "I believe in God the Father, Almighty!" Apart from the revelation of the Trinity and the Incarnation, it is possible to know *that* God is but not *who* God is.

My aim in this chapter is to explore the implications of both the yes and the no I've just given in my answer to this question. I'll look first at some of the common language and similar concepts Christians and Muslims employ when they speak about God. Then, in the next section, I'll take up again the discussion of the Trinity in an effort to see what is really at stake in this teaching. Finally, I'll review the ground we've traveled and summarize my argument before exploring in the next chapter how Jesus Christ is understood in both Christianity and Islam.

Is Monotheism Enough?

The word *Allah* is found 2,685 times in the Quran. Muhammad did not invent this word. In fact, it was the common word of address for God used by Arabic Christians centuries before Muhammad was born. Millions of Arabic-speaking Christians still address God as Allah today. In some places in the world, such as Malaysia, Muslim authorities have ordered Arabic-speaking Christians not to do so, lest the Christians' "Allah" be confused in the popular mind with the Allah of Islam. This controversial policy ignores the historical fact that Christians called God Allah long before Muslims did, as well as the Quranic affirmation that Christians and Muslims have the same God (29:46). It is a reminder, however, of the confusion that arises when we ignore either the convergence of or the contrast between differing conceptions of the one God passionately professed in both Islam and Christianity.

Allah is the contraction of two Arabic words, *il* and *ilah*—"the god." *Allah* was commonly used in pre-Islamic Arabia, sometimes associated with an individual's personal name. For example, Muhammad was the son of Abdullah, which means "the servant of Allah." The *Kabah* in Mecca was the shrine of Allah—acknowledged as a "high god" above many lesser gods; by the time of Muhammad, however, the worship of Allah had become thoroughly paganized. As we have seen, this pre-Islamic pagan Allah was believed to have engendered three "daughters" who were worshiped as goddesses, along with the stone-god, the moon-god, the pigeon-god, and numerous other deities. Muhammad broke decisively with this polytheistic confusion. He called on people to believe in Allah, not as the greatest deity in the Meccan pantheon, but as the one and only God there is. Islam began, then, as a vigorous return to an uncompromising monotheism.

When Christians read the Quran, they are often struck with how similar the Quran's depiction of God sounds to that of the Bible. For example, in the closing verses of *surah* 59, God is described as omniscient, compassionate, and merciful:

> He is God, besides whom there is no other deity. He is the sovereign Lord, the Holy One, the Giver of Peace, the Keeper of Faith; the Guardian, the Mighty One, the All-Powerful, the Most High! Exalted be God above their idols! He is God, the Creator, the Originator, the Modeller. His are the most gracious names. All that is in the heavens and the earth gives glory to him. He is the Mighty, the Wise One.
>
> 59:22–24

To which all Bible-believing Christians would surely say, "Amen!"

Again and again God is portrayed in the Quran as majestic, glorious, the Mighty One, the Wise One, the Supreme One. "Nothing," says the Quran, "can be compared with him. He alone hears all and sees all. His are the keys of the heavens and the earth. He has knowledge of all things" (42:11–12). It is sometimes asked whether Christians can learn anything from people of other faiths. The Muslim doctrine of God, in its commitment to God's utter majesty and his sovereignty over all creation, clearly has something profoundly important to teach certain Christian theologians who (contrary to what Christians have always believed) deny God's absolute knowledge of all future events. In a similar vein, others see God as a victim caught in the processes of nature and history rather than as the eternal Lord of space and time.

Muslims are told that the most beautiful names belong to God and that these names are to be used when calling on him. Islamic tradition has identified ninety-nine such names, which Muslims recite as they touch the ninety-nine beads of the rosary. These names include the First, the Last, the Forgiver, the Provider, the Truth, the Magnificent, the Sublime, the Amicable, the Nourisher, the Forbearing, the Near, and the Light. Rightly understood, as they can be from the perspective of biblical faith, all ninety-nine of the beautiful names of God in Islam are beautiful for Christians as well. They are qualities of God stressed in the Bible long before Muhammad was born or the Islamic community came into being.

How are we to explain the overlapping content between the God of Muhammad and the God who reveals himself to us in the Bible? If we do not believe—as Christians don't—that the Quran is a literal transcript of an infallible book conveyed to Muhammad by the angel Gabriel, there are at least two other ways of accounting for the fact that Islam does teach many true and important things about God. First of all, Abraham may have passed on to Ishmael and his descendants after him the special revelation God had given him, including a monotheistic belief in a creator God who must be worshiped. There were other monotheists in Arabia before Muhammad (including a group called *hanifs*) who anticipated his disdain for idolatry and harked back to the true faith of Abraham. Some have suggested that the Magi who came from Persia to worship the Messiah at Bethlehem (Matthew 2:1–12) may have belonged to another strand of this family of believers in the one God.

> *Muslims are told that the most beautiful names belong to God.*

Furthermore, we cannot rule out the possibility of contact with and borrowing from the Old Testament itself, given the presence of Christians and Jews in the Arabian world. Carl F. H. Henry notes both the genuine nature of this revelation and its limitation:

> In the post-Christian era, Muhammad gave fresh impetus to the lost abstract monotheism of the non-Hebrew world. To be sure, his emphasis that there is no God but Allah leans heavily on the Mosaic revelation. But an obscure doctrine of revelation crowds out the living monotheism of the Old Testament and allows Muhammad to emerge as Allah's prophet; moreover it clouds the dynamic monotheism of the New Testament by displacing the revelation of the supremacy and deity of Jesus Christ.[1]

But even apart from channels of special revelation, it is evident from Scripture that fallen human beings can and do know many true things about God on the basis of his general revelation in both the conscience within and the cosmos without. This natural knowledge of God has been shattered, and the image of God in human beings horribly effaced, by the effects of the Fall. But these things have not been completely destroyed. We are reminded of the common humanity we share with all persons made in the image of God. We are able to work together for justice and civility in a world of sin and violence. We can hear and follow the call to be co-belligerents in the struggle for the sanctity of life and in other pressing issues of moral concern, even with those who do not share our core convictions about God, Jesus Christ, and the Bible.

No one is exempt from this primordial awareness of God, not even the atheist who denies God's existence. As the medieval theologian Anselm argued long ago, even the fool who says in his heart, "There is no God," must have some certain idea of God beyond mere fantasy. If he didn't, his denial would be nonsense. This innate God-consciousness, which all persons possess, reminds us of this fact: We all face an ultimate accountability for the stewardship of our lives.

Paul's encounter with the religious leaders of Athens on Mars Hill has much to teach us about our approach to persons of other faiths. In the account of Paul's visit to Athens (Acts 17) we find a model of interreligious dialogue and Christian witness at the same time. Unlike certain religious pluralists today, Paul did not assume that all the various forms of religious devotion he observed were equally valid pathways to the same God. No, he was "greatly distressed" (Acts 17:16) by the flea market of idols he encountered in this city. When he preached about Jesus and the resurrection, some of his hearers thought he was proposing the addition of two new deities to the already overcrowded pantheon of Athens—which led Paul into a "dialogue" about the nature of the true God he believed in, the God who raised Jesus from the dead.

Significantly, Paul did not begin his discourse by bashing the "false gods" of the Athenians, though elsewhere his preaching did result in iconoclastic riots (see Acts 19:23–41). He began instead by identifying that which was missing in the religious worldview of his conversation partners. The fact that the Athenians had built an altar to "an unknown god" (Acts 17:23) indicated that there was a real, if unfelt, sense of inadequacy that Paul could address with the positive content of the Christian gospel. He did this by pointing precisely to the two places where God has made himself known to every person of every religious tradition, namely, the *created order* and the *human conscience*. He showed great sensitivity in quoting, not the inspired Old Testament, as he always did when speaking to Jews, but the pagan poets who were familiar to the Greeks. Of course, he did not give a stamp of approval to everything these poets had said. But he found in their writings true statements that confirmed what the Bible teaches about human beings and their relationship to God. He did not hesitate to use these non-Christian sources in his evangelistic appeal. But neither did he stop with this acknowledgment of common ground. He went on to tell them who Jesus was in relation to the God of creation. He preached Jesus Christ crucified, risen, and coming again. He pointed toward the day of judgment and called for a decision. He called on his listeners to repent and to believe the gospel. Several responded to his appeal and became Jesus-followers.

Most orthodox Muslims would have no problem with much of Paul's sermon on Mars Hill: God is the Creator and sovereign Lord of history; God is both transcendent and immanent; there will be a final judgment. But the point about God raising Jesus from the dead introduces a deep divergence that cannot be explained away as a mere historical dispute about what happened on Good Friday and Easter Sunday. This difference has important implications for how we understand the reality of God himself. Christianity and Islam cannot simply embrace one another as "sister religions" on the basis of a shared monotheism without regard to questions about Jesus and his cross and resurrection—issues in turn that presuppose further questions about Jesus and his relationship to God.

We might frame the issue another way: *Is monotheism enough?* If we assume that the God of the Bible and Allah in Islam are not two separate gods but the same God differently understood (as many Muslims who have become Christians explain their own conversion to Christ), we must still say no to the question, "Is the Father of Jesus the God of Muhammad?"

Kenneth Cragg helps sort out this difficulty. He notes that Muslims and Christians speak of the same *subject* when they speak of God, but they differ widely in the *predicates* they say about him.[2] Of course, as we have seen, Christians and Muslims do share in common a number of predicates about God—the ninety-nine beautiful names, for example. But Christians predicate something essential and irreducible about God that no Muslim can accept: *We call him our heavenly Father.* Bilquis Sheikh was a Pakistani woman of noble birth who had been a Muslim all her life. Through a series of dreams and strange encounters, she came to know and believe in Jesus Christ as her personal Savior and Lord. Quite appropriately, she titled the story of her conversion *I Dared to Call Him Father.*[3] Why would this word for God be more than a symbolic designation that Christians might just as well do without? We must go on to ask the question, "Does God need a Son?"

Does God Need a Son?

Around the side of the beautiful Dome of the Rock in Jerusalem, written in Arabic, are the words *God has no son*. Facing, as it does, the Church of the Holy Sepulchre, no other expression could illustrate so pointedly the one fundamental difference between Christianity and Islam. To this inscription the New Testament responds in the words God declares at the baptism of Jesus: "This is my Son, whom I love" (Matthew 3:17). In the Jordan River that day, the Father spoke his words of love, the Son received his approval, and the Holy Spirit descended from above to rest on Jesus.

This was a brief illustration—a visible disclosure, if we can think of it that way—of the interchange of holy love and fellowship that God has forever known within himself in the mystery of the divine Trinity. How did the church come to recognize in this insight the heart of the gospel itself?

Two Dangers

Most Christians think about the Trinity (when they do think about it) in terms of how the Trinity is related to salvation—how it affects *us*, what it has to do with *our* coming to faith. The Father sends the Son into the world; the Son of God bears our sins on the cross; the Holy Spirit gives us new life in Jesus Christ. Theologians refer to this as the "economic Trinity." It speaks of how God works outside of himself to accomplish his purposes in creation and redemption, of how he fulfills his will in history and providence. Because this salvation history is so much of what the Bible is about, it is right and good that we focus our attention here.

But there is another aspect to the reality of God—the "ontological Trinity"—that refers to who God is within himself. We must proceed with great caution here, because there are many things about the inner life of God in eternity we do not know. It is well to remember a statement made by the German religious reformer Philipp Melanchthon: "We do better to adore the mysteries of Deity than to investigate them."[4] But if what God does is unrelated to who he is, can we really trust him? In John 17:3, the economic Trinity and the ontological Trinity are brought together in a single verse: "Now this is eternal life: that they may know you, the only true God, and Jesus Christ, whom you have sent." The God who wills to be known and the Christ who has been sent to make him known belong inseparably together—which is why Jesus can say with such boldness what no other religious leader has ever dared to claim: "Anyone who has seen me has seen the Father" (John 14:9).

In seeking to understand the relationship of Jesus Christ to the Father who had sent him, the early church faced two Christological dangers. These dangers did, in fact, precipitate a crisis in the doctrine of the Trinity. The first was *modalism*—a view that says the Trinity is three different modes or masks that God wears at different times in salvation history. In the Old Testament he appeared as the Father, in the New Testament as the Son, and now, in the age of the church, we experience God as the Holy Spirit. Not only does this view contradict the witness of Scripture (for example, Jesus prays to the Father while on earth), it also eliminates the possibility of relationship within the Godhead. How could the Father "send" the Son if there is no distinction between them?

> *If what God does is unrelated to who he is, can we really trust him?*

If modalism eliminates self-distinction within God, then *subordinationism* (the opposite danger) undercuts the unity of God. Here the Son and the Spirit are agents of the Father, but they do not share in his essential oneness. The most extreme form of subordinationism was taught by Arius, who claimed that the Son/Logos was a creature made by God—an exalted creature to be sure, perhaps the greatest creature of all, but a creature nonetheless. The teaching of Arius brought about the Council of Nicaea in A.D. 325.

Arius versus Athanasius

Athanasius served as the bishop of Alexandria in Egypt. Arius was a presbyter (priest or elder) in his church. The conflict between the two became so intense that all the bishops in the Christian world were summoned to a gathering at Nicaea in 325 to resolve this dispute. There they formulated a creed, which, with a few subsequent changes, Christian churches all over the world still recite. On the crucial point of contention between Arius and Athanasius, the Nicene Creed said this:

> And in one Lord Jesus Christ,
> the only begotten Son of God,
> begotten of his Father before all worlds,
> God of God, Light of Light,
> very God of very God,
> begotten, not made,
> being of one substance with the Father.[5]

This definition flew in the face of Arius's understanding of God. To say that the Son was *homoousios*—of the same substance as the Father—was to introduce plurality and division into the Godhead. It was to be guilty of what was later described in Islam as *shirk*, that is, "associating" something that is not God with God. But why is this? Because God's innermost being or essence, according to Arius, cannot be shared, or even communicated, with anyone else. "We know," Arius said, "there is one God, alone unbegotten, alone eternal, alone without beginning, alone true, alone immortal."[6]

To this way of thinking, God is the Alone with the Alone. He is utterly transcendent, self-sufficient, and all-powerful in every way. He guards his divinity jealously, in the same way that Silas Marner guarded his gold in George Eliot's famous novel. Silas Marner was a miser who kept a chest of gold coins under his bed. Every night before he went to sleep, he would take out his gold coins, count them, stroke them, and admire them. Then he would put them back under his bed and go to sleep. He never spent any of his coins, for they were *his*. They were not to be shared with anyone else. Arius believed in a "Silas Marner" kind of God—a God wealthy beyond measure, a God so self-contained in his absoluteness that the very thought of having to share his inner-most reality, his "essence," with anyone else, even with a "son," was anathema to him.

One of the prime arguments against Arius's view was that it left the church with a Christ who was not worthy to be worshiped. If Jesus was less than fully divine, it would be idolatrous to wor-ship him. The Lord has clearly said, "You shall have no other gods before me" (Exodus 20:3). This is precisely the point made by Muslims as well—that nothing other than God can be worshiped —and they would be right in pressing it if indeed Jesus was less than fully divine.

Athanasius made the further point that if Jesus was not *homoousios* with the Father, then he could not be the Savior of the world. Arius had ridiculed the idea that God could "beget" a son. After all, everyone knows that God is above all carnal pro-creation and does not reproduce sexually, just as the Quran also declares: "God is one, the eternal God. He begot none, nor was he begotten. None is equal to him" (112:1–4).

Athanasius (and the theologians in the Nicene tradition who followed him) sought to explain the "begottenness" of the Son in a way that avoided both the sterility of Arius's Silas Marner-like God and the crass literalism derived from Greek mythology. The Nicene formula had described the Son as both the *same* in sub-stance with the Father and yet in some way also *distinct from* the Father: He was God *of (from)* God, Light *of (from)* Light, very God *of (from)* very God. The challenge was how to explain this from-ness without violating the same-ness, which they did by declaring that the Son was begotten—but not in the way that human fathers beget or generate their earthly children. No, the Son of the heavenly Father was begotten *from all eternity*. He did not "come to be" at a point in time. In fact, there never was a time when he was not. But from eternity the Father and the Son have always existed in "a relationship of total and mutual self-giving."[7]

A Unity of Love

Clearly this kind of eternal begetting would not be possible if the Father was selfish with his glory, his power, and his majesty. On the contrary, however, he is unspeakably generous. He gives all of these to the Son in an eternal interchange of holy love. Neither is the Son "self-seeking" (1 Corinthians 13:5) but returns all that he has received to the glory of the Father, with the Holy Spirit as the bond of unity between the two. The mystery of God's unity is thus *a unity of love*. When we peer into the heart of God, we find not solitary absoluteness—the Alone with the Alone—but the mystery of eternal love and relationship, a begetting without a beginning and an indwelling without an ending.

But how do we know this? Not by looking from a distance at God's majestic power and his faithful governance of the universe, nor indeed by reflecting on the awareness we have of God within our conscience. As I've observed, general revelation tells us *that* God is but not *who* God is. Only from God's self-revelation in the history of Israel and in the event of Jesus Christ do we learn the nature of the "unknown god" who is sought after and hinted at in the many religions and cultures of the world.

Athanasius pointed to a number of texts in John's gospel where the mutual self-giving between the Father and the Son is explicitly stated. John 3:35 tells us that "the Father loves the Son and has placed everything in his hands." Or again, "For as the Father has life in himself, so he has granted the Son to have life in himself" (5:26). For his part, the Son does not seek his own will but the will of the Father who sent him (see 5:30). He does nothing on his own authority but declares that which the Father has taught him (see 8:28). Because this is true, Jesus can make those remarkable statements about he and the Father being one and about

> *When we peer into the heart of God, we find the mystery of eternal love and relationship.*

how knowing him issues in knowing the Father as well (see 10:30; 14:7). And it's why Jesus can say that when people believe in him, they believe not just in him but in the one who sent him (see 12:44).

What this all means is this: What we see in the life and ministry of Jesus, including his being delivered up by the Father to the death of the cross, is *not* an aberration; it is *not* an accident. It is the revelation of who God really is—the one the New Testament calls "the God and Father of our Lord Jesus Christ" (Ephesians 1:3).

Five Implications

Bare monotheism divorced from the rich content of biblical faith is not enough. The doctrine of the Trinity is not peripheral but essential to our understanding of the character and nature of the one true God. Note the following implications that result from reflecting on the development of this doctrine in the early church:

God Is One but Not Alone

The doctrine of the Trinity does not destroy but rather reinforces God's unity. In the eternal and blessed intercommunion of the Father, the Son, and the Holy Spirit, the one true God is united without confusion and divided without separation. In Islam there are two aspects to the principle of *tawhid:* (1) oneness as opposed to idolatry, and (2) oneness as defined by solitariness within the being of God—that is, unitarianism. The first aspect of God's oneness is illustrated by the words the poet John Milton places on the lips of the father of Samson—a sentiment shared by Islam and Christianity alike:

> With cause this hope relieves thee, and these words
> I as a Prophecy receive: for God,
> Nothing more certain, will not long defer
> To vindicate the glory of his name
> Against all competition, nor will long
> Endure it, doubtful whether God be Lord
> Or Dagon.[8]

Real faith in the true God cannot coexist with idolatry, for indeed "there is no god but God." But the one true God does not exist in static isolation, the Alone with the Alone. He lives instead in the fulsome fellowship of three divine persons eternally united in being, relationship, and love. Unitarianisms of all kinds reduce the unity of God to a unit. A bare unity is always barren. In the biblical view, relationship is *constitutive* for God himself: The Father *gives,* the Son obediently *receives,* and the Holy Spirit *proceeds* from both of them.

God Is Love

It is sometimes said that Christianity is a religion of love and Islam is a religion of fear. This, however, ignores the fact that one of the ninety-nine beautiful names for God is *al-Wadud* (He Who Loves). God's love is explicitly mentioned in fifteen *surahs* of the Quran. Moreover, every *surah* except one begins with the words, "In the name of God, the Compassionate, the Merciful." The contrast lies elsewhere: In the Quran, God's love is conditional and accidental. Love is something God *does,* not that which God *is.* The conditional nature of God's love is observed in verses such as this one: "Surely for those who believe and do good deeds will Allah bring about love" (19:96).[9]

When the New Testament declares that God is love, it is saying something other than the fact that God relates to us in a loving way—though this statement is most assuredly true. As Kenneth Cragg explains, the names of God in Islam describe God's activity but not his essence: "God acts towards mankind in mercy, compassion, tenderness, might, judgment. He is not, however, 'identifiable' with or by any of these. He retains an untrammeled freedom over against any sort of moral or spiritual necessity. Man may hope for his mercy but cannot have it ensured to him. God may relate as 'loving'; he may not be said to *be* love."[10]

Note that this is a far different reading from what we find in the New Testament. In the Christian faith, God's love is neither conditional nor accidental. While we were still sinners, God loved us and Christ died for us. In fact, the good news of the gospel is precisely *not* that *we* loved God, but that he loved us and sent his Son to be an atoning sacrifice for our sins (Romans 5:8; 1 John 4:10).

God Is Free to Be Gracious

The bold statement "God is love" has many implications, one of which we see more clearly by asking the age-old question, "Why did God create the world?" According to an ancient Jewish midrash current in Jesus' day, God made the world because he needed to have a partner on whom he could bestow love. Love, by definition, requires an object. It must be directed toward something or someone else. We sometimes hear the same idea in popular Christian piety: "Once upon a time back in eternity God said, 'I'm so lonely. I think I'll create the universe so there'll be something for me to love.'"[11] Islam has a version of this same motif. In a well-known *hadith,* God is acknowledged as saying, "I was a hidden treasure; I wanted to be known. Hence I created the world so that I would be known."[12]

All of these sources tell the same story: God created the world in order to fill some deep deficiency within his own being, in order to actualize some latent possibility that otherwise would not have come true. It is precisely this kind of thinking that gives rise to process theology—the doctrine of a "limited" God who "needs" the cosmos (or humanity, in some versions of process theology) in order to actualize his own reality. This view of a disabled, transcendence-starved deity contradicts the orthodox doctrine of God in Judaism and Islam, no less than in Christianity.

But only the doctrine of the Trinity can give a credible response to this approach. Here God does not need to create the world in order to have something to love. No, he *is* love! Had God never made the world at all, he would have suffered no deficiency. Nor would he have ever been any less loving than he is now. God was never lonely. He was never locked up in solitary confinement. Ever within himself from all eternity, God is the one whose eternal unity is marked by a dynamic reciprocity, a mutuality, a holy community of love.

If all this is true, the question remains: Why *did* God create the world? The answer given by Trinitarian faith is this: Not because he had to, but because in the majestic freedom of his divine being, he *chose* to. And this decision itself, this commitment to create, and then redeem through the sharing of his Son, was not a whimsical decision made by God on the spur of the moment, as it were. It was, rather, a reflection of his own inner life and his love from all eternity. Theologian Karl Barth expressed this thought very well:

> God loves, and to do so, he does not need any being distinct from his own as the object of his love. If he loves the world and us, this is a free overflowing of the love in which he is and is God and with which he is not content, although he might be, since neither the world nor ourselves are indispensable to his love and therefore to his being. Thus the love of God is free, majestic, eternal love. . . . It is the eternal love in whose free and non-obligatory overflowing we are loved. And it is God himself in all the depths of his deity who summons and impels us to love.[13]

God is the one who is free to be gracious. This is a humbling thought for us human beings, who are so accustomed to placing ourselves at the center of the universe. This truth tells us that we are not necessary. That we are utterly contingent. That God does not "need" us in order to be God. But, paradoxically, this is also the truth that makes the Good News genuinely good. God has *chosen* to love us on the basis of his own free will and not out of coercion or necessity. With full intentionality he has decided not to remain a divine cocoon within himself. He has chosen to make a world apart from himself, to become a part of that world, and to take upon himself the burden of loving it back to himself. This he has done as a humbly born baby in a manger, as a suffering man on a cross.

> *God has chosen to love us on the basis of his own free will.*

God Is Personal

The doctrine of the Trinity tells us that relationality—personality—is at the heart of the universe. Thomas Hardy once referred to God as "a dreaming, dark, dumb Thing that turns the handle of this idle show."[14] Thomas Hardy's God is a thing, devoid of relationships. It is dark, speechless, obscure, and remote. Of course, this is a hideous caricature of the real God, but it is a caricature widely accepted in today's world. The roots of modern atheism can be traced to reaction to this kind of God—which is why the true alternative to Christian Trinitarian theology today is not competing monotheisms but atheism.

In Jesus Christ we are given to know that God is eternally love—and that he is ultimately personal.[15] True, Trinitarian theology has always struggled to understand and express the threeness of the one God. The Western church preferred *persons,* the Eastern church *substances,* Augustine favored *relations,* while Calvin preferred *subsistencies.* None of these words say perfectly everything that needs to be said. They all draw on human analogies that ultimately break down. The mystery of the God we serve remains infinitely beyond all our efforts to describe him with our broken concepts and finite words. Islamic theology (along with other theologies of reticence) is right to be wary of human efforts to define and circumscribe God. But Christian theology boldly makes this attempt, not out of irreverent curiosity or speculation, but because *this is how God has revealed himself to be.* In Jesus Christ we are confronted, not with a demigod, nor with a creature elevated to a quasi-divine status, but with the real thing: God of God, Light of Light, very God of very God.

Theologians such as John of Damascus later came to use the beautiful Greek word *perichoresis* to describe the personality and mutuality of the three divine "Persons," one with the other:

> They are inseparable and cannot part from one another, but keep to their separate courses within one another, without coalescing or mingling, but cleaving to each other. For the Son is in the Father and the Spirit: and the Spirit in the

Father and the Son: and the Father in the Son and the Spirit, but there is no coalescence or commingling or confusion. And there is one in the same motion: For there is one impulse and one motion of the three subsistences, which is not to be observed in any created nature.[16]

What this means is this: The God at the heart of the universe is not Aristotle's Prime Mover, an Uncaused Cause imprisoned in his own static aloneness. Nor is this God three individual "selves," each impervious to the needs and reality of the others. The Christian God is an unbroken unity of infinite intimacy and holy love.

God Is Sufficiently Sovereign to Come As Well As to Send

The original Muslim disallowance of the Trinity may well have been a reaction to heretical notions of tritheism, a view of God that no orthodox Christian could accept. But it is also true that even orthodox Christian teaching about the Trinity has been rejected by Islam because it has seemed to be a breach of God's sovereignty as well as of divine unity. But is this really so? Is the almightiness of God displayed only in his ability to act as a tyrant, to smash and destroy and dominate by brute force? In one of his Christmas sermons, German reformer Martin Luther once said that if he had been God, he would have brought the devil in, twisted his nose, and vanquished him on the spot. But God is amazing, Luther declares. He appears on earth in the form of a newborn baby, weak as an earthworm. And all hell trembles at his sight.

> *God appears on earth in the form of a newborn baby. And all hell trembles at his sight.*

Christians believe that God is sovereign enough not only to send his word through his prophets but also to come himself in the person of his Son. And in having done so he was perfectly consistent with his own divine nature. Arthur McGill expressed it so well:

God's divinity does not consist in his ability to push things around, to make and break, to impose his will from the security of some heavenly remoteness, and to sit in grandeur while all the world does his bidding. Far from staying above the world, he sends his own glory into it. Far from imposing, he invites and persuades. Far from demanding service from men in order to enhance himself, he gives his life in service to men for their enhancement. But God acts toward the world in this way because within himself he is a life of self-giving.[17]

A Brief Summary

It is now time to look back over the ground we've traveled in the last two chapters. While the doctrine of the Trinity has often been neglected in Christian theology and worship, it is the necessary framework for understanding who God is and how he has made himself known to us. The doctrine of the Trinity is the blueprint on which the Christian faith is built, or, to change metaphors, it is the theological genetic code that sets the limits and defines the shape of Christian doctrine. Christianity and Islam have always been at odds over the doctrine of the Trinity—and they remain so today. Some of the differences, however, have resulted from misperceptions and false interpretations. We should not be surprised, then, when Muslims misunderstand the Trinity, for all Christians acknowledge its mystery and many Trinitarian heresies have flourished under the Christian banner.

The doctrine of the Trinity is the result of Christian reflection on the history of salvation. How could the Old Testament affirmation "God is one" be reconciled with the New Testament confession "Jesus is Lord," together with the early Christian experience of the Holy Spirit as truly God, no less than the Son and the Father? Each of these affirmations was subject to great controversy and debate. Marcion questioned the unity of God by lopping off the entire Old Testament revelation. Arius undermined the deity of Jesus by claiming that he was a mere creature made by God at a certain point in time. Others conceive of the Holy Spirit as a force or energy, refusing thereby to recognize his full personhood. Eventually these conflicts found resolution in the Nicene Creed, which declared the Son to be of the same essence as the Father. This formula was a great advance over both the radical subordinationism of Arius, which denied the deity of Jesus Christ, and various forms of modalism, which disallowed any self-differentiation within the Godhead.

The Nicene debates focused on the nature of the God we worship—the issue that is at stake in the Christian conversation with Islam. Christians and Muslims together can affirm many important truths about God—his oneness, eternity, power, majesty, and so forth. Many of the names and attributes of God found in the Quran are faithful to the biblical portrayal of God—"the Living, the Everlasting, the All-High, the All-Glorious" (2:256). But Muslim theology rejects the deity of Jesus Christ and the personhood of the Holy Spirit—both of which are essential components of the Christian understanding of God. What's more, no devout Muslim can call the God of Muhammad "Father," for this, it is thought, would compromise divine transcendence. But no faithful Christian can refuse to confess, with the utmost joy and confidence, "I believe in God the Father, Almighty." Apart from the revelation of the Incarnation and the Trinity, we can know *that* God is but not *who* God is.

I concluded this chapter on the Trinity by examining five implications of this doctrine for Christian theology seen in the light of Islam. The self-disclosure of God as the Father, the Son, and the Holy Spirit—the One and the Three, united without confusion and divided without separation—shows us that God is one but not alone; God is love; God is free to be gracious; God is personal; and God is sufficiently sovereign to come as well as to send. This is the God we encounter concretely in Jesus Christ. In the next chapter I'll probe the various ways his life, vocation, and destiny have been interpreted in the world of Islam.

CHAPTER FIVE

JESUS WITH FRECKLES?

There's one God and only one, and one Priest-Mediator between God and us—Jesus, who offered himself in exchange for everyone held captive by sin, to set them all free.

PAUL, IN 1 TIMOTHY 2:5 (THE MESSAGE)

As there is only one God, so there can be only one Gospel. If God has really done something in Christ on which the salvation of the world depends, and if he has made it known, then it is a Christian duty to be intolerant of everything which ignores, denies, or explains it away.

JAMES DENNEY

Intolerant? Scottish theologian James Denney could hardly have chosen an uglier-sounding word to describe legitimate loyalty to the gospel of Jesus Christ. *Intolerant* connotes prejudiced, bigoted, insensitive to the thoughts and beliefs of others, perhaps even dangerous. Timothy McVeigh is intolerant; Osama bin Laden is intolerant. Intolerance is not something we should be commending as a virtue, is it?

There are good reasons for recoiling from embracing this word without some qualification. We know from history, as well as from current events, what religious intolerance is capable of. In the sixteenth century, less than a hundred years after both Jews and Muslims were expelled by force from Spain, a Spanish physician-theologian named Michael Servetus was put to death for stubbornly refusing to believe in the doctrine of the Trinity. In 1553, Servetus was burned in effigy by the Catholics (and in reality by the Protestants), although it could just as well have been the other way around had his journey ended in Rome rather than Geneva. Islam has its own Servetus to remember. In 922, the Sufi mystic and teacher al-Hallaj was crucified in Baghdad for having said, "I am the Truth." We can still hear the shrieks and feel the flames of the inquisitorial spirit.

> *We are not at liberty to be indifferent about the claims of the sole mediatorship of Jesus.*

Something of this same spirit lives on, it seems, in the way some Christians blithely, almost gleefully, consign their fellow human beings to the fires of hell with all the smugness of the Pharisee in the temple: "God, I thank you that I am not like other men" (Luke 18:11). Where is the compassion of Jesus in this? Where are our evangelical tears?

We are right to reject this kind of intolerance. It treats the truth of the gospel as a possession to be prized rather than as a gift to be shared. But James Denney had in mind an intolerance of a different kind. We might call it a "holy intolerance," holy because it is held humbly and in conformity to the Christ whose final miracle before his death was to heal a wound caused by one of his own disciples. The "one Gospel" Denney refers to is rooted in the conviction that Jesus is not only the Savior of the world but also the criterion by which all other truth-claims—religious and nonreligious alike—must be judged. This is what the great missionary-theologian Lesslie Newbigin called "the open secret," the fact that

Jesus Christ is not only God's truth "for me" but for all persons everywhere.[1]

In our encounter with Islam, as well as with any other world religion, we are not at liberty to be indifferent about the claims of the sole mediatorship of Jesus Christ. Two examples from recent history help show how this principle applies to the different images of Jesus in the Quran and in the New Testament.

During the early days of the Third Reich, faithful Christians in Germany were confronted with the blatant paganism oozing out of Hitler's Nazi ideology. Hitler was prepared to allow the church to do its own thing, as long as it would "be tolerant of" the claims of ultimacy made by the Nazi state. In a time of great struggle, Karl Barth led faithful Christians in Germany to make this confession, now known as the Barmen Declaration:

> Jesus Christ, as he is testified to us in the Holy Scripture, is the one Word of God, whom we are to hear, whom we are to trust and obey in life and death. We repudiate the false teaching that the church can and must recognize yet other happenings and powers, images and truths as divine revelation alongside this one Word of God, as a source of her preaching.[2]

Now be sure to notice that this statement contains both a positive affirmation and a negative clarification. Had Barth and his friends been willing to stop before getting to the second part, the Nazis may well have left them alone. It was the refusal to recognize "other happenings and powers, images and truths" as equivalent to the one and only Word of God, Jesus Christ, that led Karl Barth to be expelled, Martin Niemöller imprisoned, and Dietrich Bonhoeffer executed.

The second example—a statement by Pope John Paul II—compares Christianity and Islam. Consider two thoughts before we look at the statement. *First, by no means is Islam comparable to Nazism!* After all, Hitler was a baptized Catholic, and almost all Nazis claimed to be good Christians. Germany was the home of Martin Luther, not Muhammad. When the Jews were driven out of Spain in 1492, they found a welcome refuge under Muslim rule in Turkey, where they were allowed to practice their religion and live free of persecution.[3] While totalitarian regimes, such as that of Idi Amin in Uganda and the Taliban in Afghanistan, have flown under the Muslim banner, history is littered with so-called Christian tyrants as well. *Second, the pope is by no means anti-Islamic!* In fact, from the perspective of most evangelicals, he, and Roman Catholicism generally, may have gone too far in affirming Muslim religiosity. Certainly John Paul II has reached out to Islam in ways that encourage interreligious dialogue. He has affirmed that Christians and Muslims hold a common belief in the one God. He has called for "a civilization of love" in which there is no room for hatred, discrimination, or violence. For this very reason, one is all the more struck by the candor and "holy intolerance" (if we may call it that) evident in the following evaluation written by John Paul II:

> Whoever knows the Old and New Testaments, and then reads the Quran, clearly sees the process *by which it completely reduces Divine Revelation*. It is impossible not to note the movement away from what God said about Himself. First in the Old Testament through the Prophets, and then finally in the New Testament through His Son. In Islam all the richness of God's self-revelation, which constitutes the heritage of the Old and New Testaments, has definitely been set aside.
>
> Some of the most beautiful names in the human language are given to the God of the Quran, but He is ultimately a God outside of the world, a God who is *only Majesty, never Emmanuel,* God-with-us. *Islam is not a religion of redemption*. There is no room for the Cross and the Resurrection. Jesus is mentioned, but only as a prophet who prepares for the last prophet, Muhammad. There is also mention of Mary, His Virgin Mother, but the tragedy of redemption is completely absent. For this reason not only the theology but also the anthropology of Islam is very distant from Christianity.[4]

This is a statement of courage, not arrogance. What is truly arrogant is the postmodernist pluralism, which, in the vain pursuit of a superficial tolerance, negotiates away the ultimate commitments by which any religion lives. This view claims that all religions are essentially saying the same thing. It says that all are headed in the same direction, simply using different symbols and rituals—none of which carry any ultimate meaning. Evangelical missiologist David Hesselgrave and Muslim scholar Khurram Murad offer a better way forward. Both agree that neither the uniqueness of the Christian gospel nor the distinctiveness of the Muslim faith should be forfeited in the interest of interreligious dialogue. They also agree that dialogue and witness belong together. The call to conversion is inherent in both Christianity and Islam.[5]

More Than a Prophet?

It's easy to engage in "God talk" at an abstract and philosophical level. But the mention of Jesus makes us face the issue head-on. Ever since Jesus first asked the disciples, "Who do people say I am?" (Mark 8:27), the answers have been varied. Who is Jesus? The New Testament itself records a myriad of answers: Elijah? Jeremiah perhaps? John the Baptist come back from the dead? A prophet? Joe the Carpenter's boy? A demon-possessed man? A rabbi? The Messiah? The Son of God? The debates about Jesus continued in the church even after his resurrection and ascension. Was he just a human being whom God called or adopted in some special way? Or was he so divine that he really wasn't human at all?

Way back in the fourth century certain Christians in Alexandria emphasized the unity of Jesus' nature as the incarnate Son of God (they were called Monophysites, which means "one-nature people"). Another view prevailed in Antioch, namely, that Jesus had two natures, one human and one divine, which were totally separate from one another (those who held this view were called Nestorians, after the man [Nestorius, a bishop of Constantinople] who championed this view). After centuries of debate, the church declared at the Council of Chalcedon in 451 that Jesus Christ was to be understood as *one person in two natures*. Still the debates continued. When Islam came on the scene in the early seventh century, its own view of Jesus was influenced by some of these competing heretical sects.

All of the other major world religions arose before the time of Jesus. When Christians speak to Jews, Buddhists, Hindus, and others about Jesus, there is really "news" to share, for (with the exception of Judaism, whose Scriptures predicted his coming) Jesus is not mentioned in any of their sacred rituals or holy books. It's a different story with regard to Islam. Jesus is mentioned in fifteen *surahs* and ninety-three verses of the Quran. Eleven times he is called the Messiah. Sixteen times he is referred to as *Isa ibn Maryam*—Jesus son of Mary. (Scholars debate why the Quran always refers to Jesus as Isa, seemingly a corruption of the Hebrew name Esau.)

Numerous descriptions of Jesus are also found in the *hadiths,* or collected sayings of Muhammad. One of the most interesting comes from an early biography of the prophet by Muhammad Ibn-Ishaq titled *Life of the Messenger of God*. In the famous Night Journey to heaven, the prophet Muhammad is said to have met Abraham, Moses, and Jesus prior to his encounter with God himself. When he was asked to describe the appearance of these great prophets, Muhammad replied that "there was no man more like himself than Abraham, while Moses was ruddy-faced, tall, curly-haired, with a hooked nose. Jesus had a reddish coloring, was of a medium height, and his face was covered with freckles."[6] Other Muslim traditions portray Jesus as ascetic in appearance, with short disheveled hair and a small face. These images of Jesus are not found in the Quran, but they have exerted a lasting influence on the Muslim imagination—especially among the Sufis (Muslim mystics), many of whom have a special devotion to Jesus as well as to Muhammad.

Here in summary form is what the Quran itself teaches about Jesus:

- Jesus is presented as a prophet *(nabi)* and an apostle *(rasul)*, one in a long line of messengers of God beginning with Adam and ending with Muhammad ("the seal of the prophets"). Jesus is declared to be no more than a prophet (5:75).
- Jesus' supernatural birth is foretold to Mary, who is declared by angels to be chosen by God "above all women everywhere" (3:42).
- Mary, still a virgin, gives birth to Jesus beneath a palm tree, which miraculously provides fresh ripe dates for her to eat (19:20–27).
- Jesus speaks as an infant from his cradle, identifying himself as a prophet and servant of God.
- Jesus is referred to as the Messiah, a title not given to Muhammad or any other prophet.
- By God's permission, Jesus does many miracles—giving sight to the blind, cleansing lepers, and bringing the dead to life again. The Quran does not record any of Jesus' nature miracles, such as his changing water into wine or stilling the storm. It does mention a story not found in the New Testament in which Jesus shapes clay into the form of a bird, breathes life into it, and sets it free (5:110).[7]
- In response to Jesus' request, God sends down a table from heaven that is meant to be "a festival for all generations" for his disciples (5:112–114). This seems to be an obscure reference to either the gospel story of the Last Supper or the feeding of the five thousand.
- Jesus foretells both his death and resurrection (although, as we will see, Muslims don't believe that either of these events took place during Jesus' life on earth; they believe these things will happen in connection with Jesus' second coming).

What are we to make of such a Jesus? Christians are struck immediately by what is denied and what is garbled, as well as by what is left out. There is no Sermon on the Mount, no parable of the lost son and loving father, no discourse on the new birth, none of the rich and gripping teachings of Jesus we find in the New Testament. While

Jesus is called prophet and Messiah in the Quran, his preexistence and incarnation are explicitly denied. "God forbid that he himself should beget a son," says the Quran (19:36). Or again, "Praise be to God who has never begotten a son; who has no partner in his kingdom" (17:111). Perhaps these texts are reacting to heretical Christologies—not to the full-blown Trinitarian understanding of God's eternally begotten beloved Son but to a false notion of Jesus Christ as someone "adopted" by God and imbued with divine status. What we have in the Quran may be "a confusion about confusions."[8] But there is little comfort to be found in a Jesus who is "no more than" a prophet, and far less than the One who came from the bosom of the Father, full of grace and truth.

> *There is little comfort to be found in a Jesus who is "no more than" a prophet.*

Just the same, we should not discount the ability of a sovereign God to use even the misconstrued picture of Jesus we have in the Quran to lead Muslims to a deeper, truer knowledge of the living Christ. Many Muslims who have become Christians tell of their fascination with the mysterious Jesus of the Quran. Often Jesus appears to such people in a vision or dream, revealing his true identity or putting them in touch with others who can share the Scriptures with them.

Some, such as Gulshan Fatima, a crippled Pakistani sixteen-year-old girl, have experienced the healing power of Jesus Christ. She acquired a translation of the Quran in Urdu, her native tongue, and began reading the passages about Jesus. She began to pray, "Oh Jesus, Son of Maryam, heal me." According to her testimony, Jesus himself appeared to her, healed her, and revealed himself to her in words she had never heard before: "I am Immanuel. I am the Way, the Truth, and the Life. I am alive, and I am soon coming. See, from today you are my witness." Gulshan Fatima had never read the Bible or met a Christian, but out of this experience she learned to pray the Lord's Prayer. She began to read the Bible. Eventually she was baptized as a believer in Jesus. Even though she had to face hostility from her family and friends, she continues to tell the story of her miraculous healing and her strange journey to Jesus Christ.[9]

Conversion stories like Fatima's (and there are many) are sometimes met with a sneer by certain Christians in the West— those who aren't used to God working in such extraordinary ways. But they are not contrary to the way God has worked in the past (consider, for example, the vision of Cornelius in Acts 10). John Calvin once said that, while *we* are bound to the ordinary means of grace God has established in the life of the church, God himself is not subject to such limitations!

The Crucial Difference

One Friday afternoon outside the gates of a crowded Jerusalem Jesus of Nazareth was put to death on a Roman cross. Even Christianity's severest critics agree with these facts: Jesus suffered under Pontius Pilate, was crucified, died, and was buried. The events leading up to Jesus' arrest, trial, and crucifixion are central in all four of the gospel accounts, which have been called passion stories with extended introductions. The cross (or death) of Jesus is mentioned in most of the twenty-seven books of the New Testament. Its reality and meaning permeate all of them. Yet Muslims deny that Jesus ever suffered and died on the cross. *There can be no Christianity without this event. There can be no Islam with it.* As the distinguished Islamic scholar Seyyed Hossein Nasr has said, the noncrucifixion of Jesus is "the one irreducible fact separating Christianity and Islam, a fact which is in reality placed there providentially to prevent a mingling of the two religions."[10]

Muslims do agree with Christians that a crucifixion took place in Jerusalem that Friday afternoon—and that it was intended for Jesus. But they teach that, at the very last minute, just before Jesus was to be impaled on the cross, God intervened on his behalf and allowed someone else (later tradition says it was Judas) to be crucified in his place. All of this is based on one key verse in the

Quran, a text that has been the subject of endless commentary and debate:

> And for their saying, "verily we have slain the Messiah, Jesus the son of Mary, an Apostle of God." Yet they slew him not and they crucified him not, but they had only his likeness. And they who differed about him were in doubt concerning him: No sure knowledge had they about him, but followed only an opinion, and they did not really slay him, but God took him up to Himself. And God is Mighty, Wise!
>
> 4:157–158

The idea that it wasn't Jesus but someone else who was crucified at Calvary first surfaced among Christian heretical teachers in the early church. It shows up in a number of Gnostic texts that present a docetic (this is from the Greek word *dokeō*, which means "to seem," or "to appear") understanding of Jesus, namely, that Jesus had no real human body capable of undergoing suffering and experiencing death. According to this view, the crucifixion was a divine ruse intended to trick the devil. Jesus did not really suffer and die but only *appeared* to do so. Jesus escaped the agony of the cross, and in one version of the story, he can be seen laughing as he looks down on the scene of crucifixion. In this third-century Gnostic text, the apostle Peter is quoted as saying the following:

> I saw him apparently being seized by them and I said: "What am I seeing, Lord? Is it really you whom they take? And are you holding on to me? And are they hammering the feet and hands of another? Who is this one above the cross who is glad and laughing?" The Savior said to me: "He whom you saw being glad and laughing above the cross is the living Jesus. But he whose hands and feet they are driving the nails in is his fleshly part, which is the substitute. They put to shame that which remained in his likeness. Look at him—and me."[11]

Unlike this Gnostic text, the Quran never denies the humanity of Jesus. But the motif of Jesus' escaping the cross while a substitute died in his place is similar.

Beyond the debate over what actually happened on Good Friday lies a deeper concern. If Jesus was a true prophet and the chosen Messiah, how could God have allowed him to suffer and die in such a shameful way? In Gethsemane Jesus prayed to the Father, "If you are willing, take this cup from me" (Luke 22:42). Muslims cannot imagine that it could have been anything other than God's will to answer Jesus' prayer by rescuing him from the evil assailants marshaled against him. In Islam's presentation of the prophets of the Old Testament—Noah, Abraham, Moses, David—they all emerged victorious over their enemies. God vindicated Jesus, so Muslims say, in an even more spectacular way: He took him directly to heaven, allowing him to bypass the shameful, wrenching pain of the cross. Thus a popular Muslim apologist has referred to the Christian version of Calvary as cruci-fiction.

> *There can be no Christianity without the event of the cross. There can be no Islam with it.*

What can Christians learn from the Muslim misinterpretation of the most important event in the history of the world? First, we should be reminded of how shocking the fact of the cross really is. Remember that Jesus' disciples themselves did not understand his own predictions about his suffering and death until after the event. Remember that Peter once rebuked Jesus at the very thought of Jesus' undergoing a degrading death. "Never, Lord!" Peter said. "This shall never happen to you!" (Matthew 16:22). The Muslim objection to the cross is not unlike that of Peter's here. It stems from loyalty to a preconceived notion of deity—a God who will not allow his chosen ones to suffer indignity, defeat, and death.

The Christian doctrine of a suffering love does not go down well in a world that worships at the shrine of success and works at denying death. We should not underestimate the appeal of the cynic who thinks that Christianity can be discredited in one fell swoop: "Point to the cross and say: 'What a way to run the universe!'"[12] A raptured Jesus, or a laughing Christ, makes much more sense than a crucified Messiah.

Second, while Christians have no trouble believing in the cross as an event of history, they have all too often acted as though the Muslim version of things were true. After the conversion of Constantine in the fourth century, the church quickly moved from being a persecuted minority to become a persecuting authority. Christians have not always been on the right side of the struggle for religious liberty or of the quest for human rights. In 1554 Menno Simons, the leader of the Dutch-speaking Anabaptists, published *The Cross of the Saints*. Many of his fellow believers had been harassed, tortured, and put to death—not by pagans or Muslims but by their fellow "Christians," all acting in the name of Jesus Christ. Menno called on his followers to face with steadfastness and courage the supreme sacrifice:

> Therefore, oh you people of God, gird yourselves and make ready for battle; not with external weapons and armor as the bloody, mad world is wont to do, but only with firm confidence, a quiet patience, and a fervent prayer. . . . The thorny crown must pierce your head and the nails your hands and feet. Your body must be scourged and your face spit upon. On Golgotha you must pause to bring your own sacrifice. Be not dismayed, for God is your captain.[13]

There are two tombs in the Muslim world that are designated for Jesus. One remains empty, while the other is reportedly filled with his mortal remains. The empty tomb is in Medina, next to the tomb of the prophet Muhammad. As I've noted, orthodox Muslims believe that Jesus was taken to heaven before Judas, or someone else, was allowed to die in his place on the cross. Jesus lives with God in heaven now, they say, but will one day return to earth to play an important role in the last days. Islam has a vivid eschatology, and according to a popular tradition, Jesus will return to earth and make an appearance either at the Grand Mosque of

Damascus or at the Dome of the Rock in Jerusalem. At that time, he will destroy all crosses to reveal that Christians should not worship him. He will also slaughter a number of pigs (an unclean animal, according to Islam), slay the antichrist, and inaugurate a forty-year messianic reign. During this time he will marry and raise a family. He will die and be buried next to Muhammad in Medina. He will then rise again at the resurrection, thus fulfilling the prophecy of the Quran (see 19:33).

A somewhat different version is told by the Ahmadiyyah movement—a sectarian branch of Islam that began in India in the late nineteenth century. This group admits that Jesus was crucified, but it claims that he was taken down from the cross before he died and later was revived in the cool atmosphere of the tomb. They believe that Jesus then traveled to the East, where he taught and lived for many years. He then died and was buried in Kashmir, where his "tomb" can still be seen today.

During his earthly ministry, Jesus warned his disciples not to be duped by pretenders and deceivers. "At that time if anyone says to you, 'Look, here is the Christ!' or, 'There he is!' do not believe it" (Matthew 24:23). By discounting God's inspired word in Holy Scripture, Islam misses the story of the real Jesus. It constructs an ephemeral Christ who neither matches the facts of history nor meets the deepest needs of the human heart. The real Jesus isn't buried in Kashmir, nor does he await a future entombment in Medina. Crucified, risen, and ascended to heaven, he still bears in his glorified body the marks of his passion. Christians also are called to bear the "brand marks" of Jesus—to live under the cross. It is the only thing we have any biblical warrant to boast about (see Galatians 6:14–17). Yes, Jesus could have escaped the bloody affair of Calvary. He could have summoned the legions of angels. He could have heeded those who said, "Come down now from the cross" (Mark 15:32), just as he could have yielded to the tempter's whisper to become a renowned success by jumping down from the highest point of the temple (see Matthew 4:5–6). But this was not the way of Trinitarian love. God so loved that he gave ... Jesus so loved that he came. In deep humility and obedience—true *islam*—Jesus gave himself over to a criminal's death on the cross.

The cross of Jesus has an amazing power to break through the deepest resistance to the gospel. Lamin Sanneh is a leading theologian and scholar of Islam. Originally from Gambia, he was brought up in a devout Muslim home and participated in all the religious disciplines, including reading the Quran. Struck by the Quran's testimony about Jesus as a prophet and an apostle of God, Sanneh was puzzled by the verse that said "somebody else" was crucified in the place of Jesus:

> I was interested in the teaching of life after death, and it struck me that if God was indeed personally involved in rescuing Jesus from the cross by taking someone else—whoever it was—and exchanging him for Jesus, as the Qur'an says, then God surely bore responsibility for the death of this nameless victim. . . .
>
> But suppose Jesus did die on the cross, and suppose God intended it to be so; how would that change our knowledge of God? I reflected on the suffering and the heartbreak which are part of life, hopes that are often dashed to pieces. . . . It seemed to me that deep down at the center and core of life, the cross and its anonymous burden was declaring something about the inner integrity and mystery of life which rang true to all authentic experience. . . .
>
> In such a case, it would follow that God actually did demonstrate his solidarity with humanity by visibly entering our world and defeating death itself, allowing us to understand life in a wholly new way, with redemptive love able to overcome human wickedness and reveal the true face of God. Seen in the light of the cross of Jesus Christ, all of human nature, indeed all of history, appears to gather at one sharp, poignant place. It all began to make sense to me. The need for the cross seemed so compelling and true to the way life is. . . .
>
> As might be expected, it was difficult to find a Christian community, and Muslim friends who felt scandalized by my

conversion abused me harshly. In these situations God showed me that the cross of Calvary is a constant, unchangeable fact which can transform our lives at every moment, whatever the situation.[14]

The True Isa

In Christian theology, the Trinity and the Incarnation belong inseparably together. It is impossible to have one without the other. By reflecting on who Jesus was and what he came to do, the early church was compelled to confess with Thomas, "My Lord and my God!" (John 20:28). This confession gives meaning to the cross; it makes the cross central in understanding the character of God, as well as in explaining the historical fate of Jesus. If Jesus is not the eternal divine Son of the Father—God of God, Light of Light, very God of very God—then what happened on Good Friday would have been no more than a minor footnote in the chronicles of late antiquity, no different from the thousands of other crucifixions that took place in the Roman world before and after the time of Jesus.

"'Tis mystery all! The Immortal dies," wrote Charles Wesley. What mystery? The mystery that the Almighty Creator of the universe could—and did—become a man in the second person of the Trinity *and that he did this without ceasing to be God;* the mystery that he could—and did—embrace the shameful death on the cross, a death he did not deserve (here the Muslim view is completely right), in order to rescue a race of sinful rebels from the consequences of their own rebellion; and, mystery of mysteries, that he would—and did—do all of this not because he had to but because he chose to, moved only by the same interpenetrating love that he, the one God, had forever shared as the Father, the Son, and the Holy Spirit.

Thus the cross is not just an isolated event back then and there, although it surely *was* an event back then and there and not just a piece of divine chicanery—but there was a cross in the heart of God before there was a cross on the hill of Golgotha. It's why God

> *There was a cross in the heart of God before there was a cross on the hill of Golgotha.*

can say to his people, "I have loved you with an everlasting love" (Jeremiah 31:3). It's why, even now, Jesus bears in heaven the scars of his passion, a witness to the triumph of the Crucified. Before such a mystery, only the questioning language of ecstasy is possible. Charles Wesley again: "Amazing love! how can it be that Thou, my God, shouldst die for me?"

This is the true Isa who meets us in the pages of the New Testament, the Jesus who seeks us out along the dusty lanes and busy roadways of life, the Isa who says to all whose burdens are no longer bearable: "Come to me, all you . . ." (Matthew 11:28). This Isa is the Jesus of the scars:

If we have never sought, we seek thee now;
Thine eyes burn through the dark, our only stars;
We must have sight of thorn-pricks on thy brow,
We must have thee, O Jesus of the scars.

The heavens frighten us; they are too calm;
In all the universe we have no place.
Our wounds are hurting us; where is the balm?
Lord Jesus, by thy scars, we know thy grace.

The other gods were strong; but thou wast weak;
They rode, but thou didst stumble to a throne;
But to our wounds only God's wounds can speak,
And not a god has wounds, but thou alone.[15]

CHAPTER SIX

GRACE FOR THE STRAIGHT PATH

Man is so prone to consider that he can earn his way with God that whether Jew or Muslim or Christian he has turned aside from the thought that God is in him to will and to do and that God is all in all and so the unmotivated grace of God is obscured and dimmed.

J. W. SWEETMAN

After considering the doctrines of God (theology) and Jesus Christ (Christology) in the previous chapters, I now want to examine the question of how the God we know in Jesus Christ is savingly related to human beings (soteriology). While this sequence—Trinity, Incarnation, salvation—makes good sense theologically, Christians in the early church experienced these realities in exactly the reversed order. First, they encountered the living presence of Jesus—the healer, prophet, exorcist, suffering servant, crucified Savior, risen Lord. Then, in reflecting on who Jesus was and what he had done, they were led to say with the Samaritan woman, "Come, see a man who told me everything I ever did. Could this be the Christ?" (John 4:29). Convinced that Jesus indeed was the Messiah, the very Word and Wisdom of God, they came to see that this made sense only in terms of the triune reality of the one God—the Father, the Son, and the Holy Spirit.

The Trinity was never a mathematical question of figuring out how *one* can really be *three,* but always a religious one of understanding relationality as the decisive mark of God's divinity. It is God the Father who sends the Spirit of his Son into our hearts, enabling us to also call God "Father" (see Galatians 4:6). This is why Christians were, and still are, baptized in the name of the one triune God—and also why Christians declared, with apostolic boldness, that salvation was to be found in "no other name under heaven" (Acts 4:12). Christians and Muslims both profess faith in the one God, but they differ strongly about the character and nature of this one God. And despite the Quran's portrayal of Jesus as God's virgin-born Messiah, his role as Savior and Lord is undercut by the hypothesis of his noncrucifixion. It will be helpful now to see why Muslims think that Jesus' death on the cross not only never happened but also was never needed. This leads us to look at the concept of salvation in these two faith traditions.

Salvation in Islam

The first *surah* of the Quran (called the *Fatihah*) has been a standard feature of Muslim worship since Muhammad first gathered a community around him in Mecca:

> In the name of God, the Compassionate, the Merciful. Praise be to God, Lord of the universe, the Compassionate, the Merciful, Sovereign of the day of judgment! You alone we worship and to You alone we turn for help. Guide us to the straight path, the path of those whom You have favored, not of those who have incurred Your wrath, nor of those who have gone astray.
>
> 1:1–7

Colin Chapman, a Christian minister and scholar of Islam, has compared the *Fatihah* to the Lord's Prayer Jesus taught his disciples. He points out striking similarities, as well as points of divergence. Rightly understood, there is nothing in the *Fatihah* that a Christian cannot pray. Chapman admits to praying the

Fatihah alongside the Lord's Prayer in his own devotions. "When I do so," he says, "it provides a way of praying *for* and *with* the Muslim world." When he comes to the words, "Guide us to the straight path," he prays that Muslims, no less than Christians, will "come to see Jesus, son of Mary, as the Way to the knowledge of God as Father."[1]

> To be a true
> Muslim
> is to be
> on the
> straight path.

But what do Muslims understand by "the straight path"? This expression is used elsewhere in the Quran to describe the entire way of Islam. "God will surely guide the faithful to a straight path" (22:54). To be a true Muslim is to be on the straight path. To be an unbeliever is to have gone astray. Now what does this mean?

The story of the human family in Islam begins with Adam, just as it does in Judaism and Christianity. Although created from clay, Adam was the crown of God's creation. God made him his deputy, or caliph, on earth. He was taught the names of all the things God had created. This knowledge Adam was granted was superior to that of the angels, whom God commanded to bow down to Adam. All of the angels obeyed except one—Iblis, as Satan is called in the Quran (2:34).

From the beginning Adam, and by inference all human beings, was endowed with an innate awareness of the divine, called *fitra*—the basis for the special stewardship entrusted to him by God.

The Quran uses two mythlike stories to explain this unique stewardship. In one account, God offered this "trust" first to the heavens and then to the mountains. But they said, "No, choose someone else." It was then that "man undertook to bear it" (33:72). The other account presents a scene known as the Covenant of Alast. God is portrayed as having gathered together the whole human family—all the descendants of Adam—to confront them with their accountability to him: "Your Lord brought forth descendants from the loins of Adam's children, and made them testify against themselves. He said: 'Am I not your Lord?'

They replied: 'We bear witness that you are.' This he did lest you should say on the Day of Resurrection: 'We had no knowledge of that'" (7:172).

Muslim theology is reluctant to describe human beings as created in the image of God because it would imply too close a connection between a mere creature and the Almighty Creator of all things. But the Covenant of Alast (*alast* is the Arabic word for "am I not?") implies that deep within every human soul lies an innate knowledge of God and a responsibility to serve him as Lord and Master. This is the true meaning of *islam,* namely, to submit to God, to serve and obey him as his chosen deputy on earth. In the words of Genesis 1:28, human beings were created to "rule over" the creation under the lordship of God.

What went wrong? Islam and Christianity agree that there was a "fall" from the primordial state of creation. But they describe this fall and its consequences very differently. The Quran says Adam forgot to walk in the right way. Sin is forgetfulness, heedlessness, a failure to remember. This forgetting to obey is the result of inherent weakness, not active rebellion against God. It is a serious breach of the primordial covenant God made with humans, but it need not do any permanent damage. Once Adam repents, as he does, God quickly forgives. From that time on, Adam lived a perfect life. God elevated him to the status of prophet. As one Muslim scholar put it, Adam was "the author of the first human mistaken ethical perception, committed with good intention, under enthusiasm for the good."[2] God's forgiveness requires no bloody sacrifice, no atonement, certainly no agony on the part of God. God simply wills it, and it is so.

If sin is forgetfulness, its proper remedy is remembrance (*dhikr* in the Quran), which is why God has sent so many prophets— 124,000 in all, from Adam to Muhammad. One of the names Muhammad used to describe himself was "warner." Through the prophets God reminds the people of his own oneness. He instructs them to walk in the straight path. Again and again, God calls them to worship him and him alone, to forsake all idols, to purify themselves of every trace of *shirk*—the horrible sin of associating some creaturely thing with God himself. According to Islam, one way to overcome the tendency to forgetfulness is to practice *Salat* (the act of ritual prayer): "Remember the name of your Lord morning and evening; in the night-time worship Him; praise Him all night long" (76:25–26). The prophets convey the law of God, a divine code of guidance for every situation of life. This is the reason Muslims are so concerned that the *shariah* (the law of God based on the Quran) be strictly applied to the legal, political, and economic structures of society, as well as be upheld in one's personal life. There is no separation of church and state, no distinction between sacred and secular. Remembrance of Allah should encompass everything human beings do, from going to war to making love, from affairs of the state to affairs of the heart. *Shariah* literally means "road" or "path." In order for the Muslim community to be truly Islamic (surrendered to God's will), this divine law must be strictly followed.

Islam teaches that God's messengers and prophets have brought the very thing forgetful and ignorant human beings most need, namely, divine guidance, the perfect distillation of which is the Quran. Obedience to God's revealed guidance is the way to salvation, and it involves both correct belief and righteous acts: "To those who believe and do deeds of righteousness hath God promised forgiveness and a great reward" (5:10). What exactly must be believed? Essentially the *Shahada:* "There is no god but God and Muhammad is the Messenger [Prophet] of God."

Reciting this confession solemnly and sincerely is the one thing necessary in order to become a Muslim. However, according to tradition, Muhammad summarized the essence of Muslim theology in terms of these six required beliefs:

1. **God.** This belief is contained in the first part of the *Shahada* but also includes God's attributes and "most beautiful names."
2. **The Angels.** Angels are God's unseen messengers, and they play a major role in the Quran. There are four archangels— including Gabriel, through whom Muhammad received his

revelations. Azrael is the angel of death and Seraphiel is the angel who will blow the trumpet at the end of time. Every human being is assigned two guardian angels, one to record the good deeds and the other the evil acts done in this life (see 82:11). The *jinn* are demonic spirits created by God out of a fiery substance. They tempt and oppress human beings throughout their lives on earth.

3. **The Books.** These are the scriptures revealed through all the prophets in the past. Many have been lost, but, in addition to the Quran, Muslims recognize the Pentateuch, the Psalms, and the Gospel as inspired by God. However, as God's final word through the last of his prophets, the Quran surpasses the Hebrew and Christian Scriptures, which have been "corrupted" and are no longer reliable.

4. **The Apostles.** This word is synonymous with "prophets," and the Quran names twenty-five of them. All but three of these are also listed in the Bible.

5. **The Last Day.** The day of final judgment when God's verdict on the final destiny of each soul will be revealed.

6. **The Decree.** God's predestination of all events, both good and evil, that come to pass. This topic has been hotly debated in Islam. Some verses in the Quran support a fatalistic interpretation; others make room for freely chosen human acts and for moral responsibility.

As important as these beliefs are, salvation in Islam is not "by faith alone." Faithful Muslims enter the straight path by reciting the *Shahada,* but they make progress toward paradise only by strenuous effort—*jihad* in the way of God—which includes all of the pillars of Islam (belief, prayer, fasting, giving alms, and pilgrimage), as well as through carrying out other religious duties and obligations. "Rule-keeping as religion" is how one scholar has characterized Islam.[3] This definition is too narrow, given the stress on inner purification, especially in mystical and folk Islam. The washing of the hands before prayer must be accompanied by the cleansing of the heart from worldly cares.[4] There is a *jihad* of the heart in Islam, as well as of the hand, the tongue, and the sword. True religion is an entire way of life, which includes the inner as well as the outer dimensions of obedience. In Islam, as in Christianity, one can be outwardly pious and inwardly deceitful, or publicly upright and privately wretched, as this story illustrates:

> The Prophet was once informed of a woman who used to offer prayers regularly and kept fasts very often. She gave alms frequently but her neighbors were sick of her abusive tongue. The Prophet said, "Such a woman deserves only the fire of hell!"[5]

But none of this diminishes the fact that, for this view of salvation, human beings are fully capable of determining their own eternal destiny by their own exertion, discipline, and devotion. Redemption is not a category Islam recognizes. Every Muslim is his or her own redeemer. Many Muslims do, however, appeal to Muhammad—and some even to Jesus—for help in fulfilling the demands of God's law.

Is there no place then for God's mercy or love in this schema? No Muslim would admit that this is the case. Indeed, one verse in the Quran describes God as turning to his people in mercy so that they might repent (9:119). But what is this merciful "turning" on God's part? Is it not the sending of the prophets, the giving of the law, the dispensing of signs to remind forgetful human beings of the straight path? And, no less important, God's love is conditioned upon a faithful response to his revealed will. The Quran says that God loves those who are pure, patient, and upright (2:222; 5:42), as well as those who fight for his cause (61:4). But there are other categories of people God is said *not* to love: aggressors (2:190), the corrupt (5:64; 28:77), the evil unbelievers (2:276), the ungrateful (22:38), the braggarts (31:18), the prodigals

> *Faithful Muslims make progress toward paradise only by strenuous effort.*

111

(6:141), the proud and boastful (4:36), the wrongdoers (3:57, 140; 42:40), the treacherous (4:107; 8:58; 22:38), those of harsh speech (4:148), the transgressors (5:87).[6] God *may* choose to pardon—to be merciful and forgive—but he may just as well choose not to do so. His forgiveness is inscrutable. There is no assurance that God will choose to forgive any particular sinner of any particular sin on the day of judgment. Even when Muhammad himself was dying, he expressed doubt about whether he would be accepted by God, although he was prepared to trust God's mercy.

Islamic theology draws on two images to describe the final judgment—the scale and the bridge. The *scale* refers to the weighing in the balance of all the good and evil deeds done in one's life. The scale will show what the guardian angels have recorded— secret thoughts as well as public acts—and every individual will face the consequences of his or her deeds. The exactness of the scale is beyond question.

The idea of the bridge is based on two verses in the Quran that speak of those who will not find God's favor treading "the path of hell" when "their very feet will testify to their misdeeds" (37:23–24; 36:66). Even those who have been on the straight path in this life must finally come to a bridge across the fire of hell. This bridge is said to be finer than a hair and sharper than a sword. The righteous will cross the bridge with the swiftness of lightning, while others will creep along in a crawl. Those whose deeds have fallen short of God's standard will lose their footing and fall into the flames beneath. Believers may appeal to Muhammad to intercede for them, but there is no assurance that God will heed his pleadings. Those who make it across the bridge without stumbling will be ushered into a paradise of sensual delights far removed from the agonies of the damned:

> Such is the paradise which the righteous have been promised: Therein shall flow rivers of water undefiled, and rivers of milk forever fresh; rivers of wine delectable to those that drink it, and rivers of clarified honey. There shall they eat of every fruit, and receive forgiveness from their

Lord. Are they to be compared to those who shall abide in hell forever, and drink scalding water which will tear their bowels?

47:15; see also 56:12–39

Despite the muted note about intercession, the Quran strongly emphasizes that everyone will reap the fruits of his or her own deeds on the day of judgment. No soul will bear another's burden (6:164). The Muslim scholar Abul A'la Maududi has described the final accounting in this way:

> Man will stand by himself—helpless and alone—to render his account, and awake the pronouncement of judgment, which shall be in the power of God alone. Judgment will rest on one question: Did man conduct himself, in submission to God, in strict conformity with the truth revealed to the prophets, and with the conviction that he would be held responsible for his conduct in life on the Day of Judgment? If the answer is in the affirmative, the reward will be paradise; if in the negative, the punishment will be hell.[7]

Is Guidance All We Need?
Salvation in Christianity

As this brief survey shows, there are clear points of convergence between the Muslim and the Christian understanding of salvation. In both views, God created human beings directly and entrusted them with a unique stewardship over all that he made. Both agree that something went wrong between humans and God. Things are different now from the way they once were—from the way things ought to be. Furthermore, God has taken the initiative to reveal his will to his human creatures. He has done this by sending messengers and revealing his law, thus giving guidance for humans to walk on the straight path, or what Jesus called in the Sermon on the Mount the "narrow" road (Matthew 7:14). Finally, human beings are accountable to God. They will one day face a definite reckoning with him. Islam and Christianity, the world's two largest faith traditions, are both religions of revelation and salvation. It is only within this common framework of meaning that we can truly appreciate the deep divergences between the straight path of Muhammad and the narrow road of Jesus.

To illuminate further, let's look at five major principles of the Christian understanding of salvation.

The Effects of the Fall Are Deep and Systemic

From Genesis to Revelation, the Bible teaches that human beings are in a mess. We are born as rebels who have inherited a corrupted nature from our parents and who grow up in an environment tainted by sin. We have all taken the *wrong* path, not the straight path. Rather than obeying God's law, we have been ruled by pride and self-interest. Men and women everywhere live under the certain reign of death and the inescapable wrath of God (see Romans 3:9–20; Ephesians 2:1–3). This is the bad news that the good news of God's grace addresses.

Muslim theology regards this "pessimism of Christian diagnosis," as one scholar called it, as unduly gloomy and self-defeating. Adam sinned, to be sure, but he was quickly forgiven when he was reminded of the error of his ways. But is ignorance the deepest dilemma of the human predicament? Can we really explain the brokenness and alienation of the human story by an atomistic view of sin that sees each act of transgression as an isolated unit unrelated to the moral lapses that came before and that will come after? Should we not rather understand sin as a contagious disease, a deep-seated self-centeredness that permeates beyond the individual transgressor and corrupts the entire human community? For indeed, "all have sinned and fall short of the glory of God" (Romans 3:23). This is what Christians mean when they speak about the deep and systemic effects of original sin. It is "original," not in the sense that

> *We need redemption, not merely revelation. We need grace, not simply guidance.*

it was Adam's sin and not mine, but in the sense that Adam's sin *is* mine! This is why "the wages of sin is death" (Romans 6:23)—both physical and spiritual—for everyone.

As Christians see it, the Muslim understanding of sin is inadequate, even on the basis of the Muslim understanding of salvation. As Fuller Seminary professor Dudley Woodberry has shown, the Quran itself depicts fallen human beings as more than merely forgetful. They are sinful (14:4), foolish (33:72), ungrateful (14:34), weak (4:28), boastful (11:9–10), quarrelsome (16:4), and rebellious (96:6). If God punished human beings for their sins, the Quran says, not one creature would be left alive! (16:61). If the human situation could be salvaged by guidance alone, why were 124,000 prophets needed instead of just one? Why did human beings who had been shown the straight path "corrupt" the God-given scriptures? Why is *shirk* such an ever-present danger in every human community? All of this suggests a tenacity, a stubbornness, about sin that guidance alone cannot remedy. We need redemption, not merely revelation. We need grace, not simply guidance.

The Holiness of God Calls for Atonement

The notion of vicarious atonement makes no sense in the Muslim scheme of things. Islam expects everyone to bear his or her own burden, not someone else's. Even if Jesus did die on the cross, what difference would it make for me? Why can't God simply forgive without a sacrifice of any kind? The doctrine of the atonement makes sense only in a context that takes seriously a holy God who abhors evil. The Quran does refer to God as "the Holy" *(al Quddes)*. But this word seems to be synonymous with transcendence, otherness, the God whose ways are not our ways, as the Bible puts it (Isaiah 55:8). While transcendence surely is an essential component of God's holiness, it is not the complete picture. In the Bible holiness connotes not only supremacy but also purity. The holiness of God is a righteous holiness that will not suffer defilement or contamination from sin.

In Muslim theology, there is a sense in which God can forgive easily because sin does not affect him deeply. How could the

Almighty God be troubled by the trifling mistakes of a mere mortal? Yet, in the Bible, God is described as becoming troubled—deeply troubled—by the sinful rebellion of the men and women he made in his image. He is offended and grieved by their sins. He is described as being angry, moved to righteous indignation. But what is truly astounding is this: Though God's eyes "are too pure to look on evil" (Habakkuk 1:13), he does not remain aloof from the world, isolated in the splendor of his holiness. He is the Holy One *"among you,"* as Isaiah says (Isaiah 12:6, emphasis added). More astounding still is this: God wants his people to share in his own holiness. He says to Israel: "You are to be holy to me because I, the LORD, am holy, and I have set you apart from the nations to be my own" (Leviticus 20:26). Or again, "Be holy, because I am holy" (Leviticus 11:44).

In the Old Testament there were sin offerings and guilt offerings and an annual Day of Atonement in which sacrifices were offered to the Lord, the God of holiness, on behalf of the people of Israel. None of these sacrifices were finally adequate, because they were all offered by sinful persons who themselves needed someone else to atone for them (see Hebrews 5:1–3). In the New Testament this sacrificial system reaches a climax with the coming of Jesus—"the Lamb of God, who takes away the sin of the world" (John 1:29). At his birth Jesus was revealed as both Immanuel—"God with us"—and "the holy one" (Matthew 1:23; Luke 1:35). On the cross Jesus did what God alone can do: He bore the cost of our sins. Why did he do this? Because he loved us dearly. How did it happen? Through Jesus' willing acceptance of the punishment we deserved. How do we get in on this? By repenting of our sins, trusting Jesus as our Savior, and following him as our Lord. This is the truth of the gospel:

> Out of sheer generosity [God] put us in right standing with himself. A pure gift. He got us out of the mess we're in and restored us to where he always wanted us to be. And he did it by means of Jesus Christ.
>
> God sacrificed Jesus on the altar of the world to clear that world of sin. Having faith in him sets us in the clear. God

decided on this course of action in full view of the public—
to set the world in the clear with himself through the sacrifice of Jesus, finally taking care of the sins he had so patiently
endured. This is not only clear, but it's *now*—this is current
history! God sets things right. He also makes it possible for
us to live in his rightness.

Romans 3:24–25 THE MESSAGE

Forgiveness Means a Restored Relationship

Ida Glaser has written an important essay on Islam and
Christianity in which she argues that the concept of relationship
is the key to a comparative understanding of these two traditions.[8] In previous chapters I've noted how this principle applies
to the nature of God and to the person and work of Jesus Christ.
Both Christians and Muslims affirm the unity of God, but Christians understand this unity in terms of a complex oneness,
namely, the one God who knows himself from all eternity as the
Father, the Son, and the Holy Spirit. God *is* love, not just in his
outward acts, but also in the holy fellowship of his own tri-
personal eternal life of self-giving. Likewise, the doctrine of Jesus
Christ is based on the idea of relationship. How else could God
himself in the person of his Son come to earth and walk among
human beings, live with them, eat with them, weep with them,
and finally die for them?

In the Middle Ages, theologians (presumably with nothing better to do) developed what they called *asinus*-theology, an ass-
theology. They asked, "Could God have become incarnate in an
ass instead of a man? Could God just as well have become a stone,
a star, or a water lily?" Some theologians answered, "Well, yes, by
means of his absolute power, God could have become absolutely
anything." The church's better theologians wisely rejected this way
of doing theology, for it was based on mere speculation and not
on God's revealed Word.

But the *asinus*-theologians did raise an important point: Why
did God become incarnate in a human being? Paul answers this
question by declaring that God did so because he desired to share

a special relationship with the human creatures made in his image:

> But when the time arrived that was set by God the Father, God sent his Son, born among us of a woman.... You can tell for sure that you are now fully adopted as his own children because God sent the Spirit of his Son into our lives crying out, "Papa! Father!"
> Galatians 4:3, 6 THE MESSAGE; see also Hebrews 4:15–16

In Islam, the Incarnation is preposterous and the cross unnecessary. Why? Because there is no possibility for human beings to share a real relationship with God in the sense that Christians understand such a relationship—not merely as a slave to a master but, far more intimately, as a son or daughter with a loving father. In speaking of Islam, Ida Glaser observes the following:

> God's love may cause him to have mercy on his creatures, even to the extent of communicating with them; but it is a love that condescends in beneficence rather than a love that shares in relationship. God may love us if he so chooses, but his relationship with the objects of his love is very different from that envisaged in the Christian faith.[9]

Why does God desire such a relationship with us? *Because this is the kind of God he is!* What we see in the cross—what we see in the atonement—is an expression of the same intra-Trinitarian love that has forever existed in the heart of God. Never are we allowed to say that God loves us because Jesus died for us. No, it's the other way around. Jesus died for us because God, in his infinite freedom, chose to set his love on us.

Forgiveness, then, is more than an easy amnesty granted by a sovereign ruler who may never again see the person he has pardoned—if indeed he's ever met him in the first place. In the Christian faith forgiveness means the healing of a broken *relationship*. It is a costly forgiveness, to be sure, for, as D. M. Baillie writes, "it comes from the heart of a love that has borne our sins and because the love is infinite, the passion is infinite too. 'Who suffers more than God?' asks Piers Plowman [in William Langland's allegorical poem *The Vision of William concerning Piers the Plowman*]. There is an atonement, an expiation, in the heart of God himself. Out of this comes the forgiveness of our sins."[10]

Because God Is Credible, Assurance Is Possible

As I've already observed, one of the most characteristic traits of Muslim spirituality is the lack of assurance when facing death or contemplating the final judgment. Umar, one of the caliphs who succeeded Muhammad, is reported to have made this statement on his deathbed: "I am none other than as a drowning man who sees possibility of escape with life, and hopeth for it, but feareth he may die and lose it, and so plungeth about with hands and feet.... Had I the whole East and West, gladly would I give up all to be delivered from this awful terror that is hanging over me."[11]

The uncertainty reflected in this deathbed story is based on the fear of a judgment yet to come. This is a judgment Christians believe has already taken place, once for all, on the cross of Calvary. Because Jesus Christ died in our place, absorbing the infinite wrath of a holy God as our sin-bearer and substitute, we no longer have to face with dread and fear the prospect of coming before God's throne. This produces great confidence and joy for the Christian believer. But we must be careful not to confuse Christian assurance with carnal assuredness. The certainty of faith does not lie in our greatness but in the crucified and risen Christ who has redeemed us.

We are not promised a certainty unmixed with doubt or a security uninterrupted by anxiety. But we can face head-on the struggles and storms of the spiritual life, trusting wholeheartedly in the merits of the Son of God, who loved us and gave himself for us (see Galatians 2:20). No one has said it better than the great religious reformer Martin Luther. "Our faith is certain," he said, "because it carries us out of ourselves, that we should not lean on our own strength, our own conscience, our own feeling, our own person, and our own works, but to that which is without us. That is to say, the promise and truth of God which cannot deceive us."[12]

New Life in Jesus Christ Brings Transformation

Because of its strong emphasis on the atoning death of Jesus Christ and the forgiveness achieved through his sacrifice on the cross, one Muslim theologian has labeled Christianity "saviorism."[13] But as important and necessary as this salvific aspect of the Christian message is, it is not the end result.

> *The Almighty God of the universe has deigned to share his innermost life with us.*

The goal of redemption is *transformation*. The transformation God intends for his children is not merely personal improvement or psychological readjustment. It is what the New Testament calls (in language that must shock any orthodox Muslim—and troubles even some Christians) *participation in the divine nature* (see 2 Peter 1:4). To Muslims this sounds like the most horrible form of *shirk* imaginable, for God's innermost being cannot even be known, much less shared with others. And, indeed, it would be the height of presumption for human beings to arrogate to themselves such a high and unimaginably glorious privilege, just as it would be useless to try to achieve such a standing by strenuous self-effort. But the good news of the gospel is this: The Almighty God of the universe has deigned to share his innermost life with us. As Eugene Peterson puts it in his translation of this passage from 2 Peter:

> Everything that goes into a life of pleasing God has been miraculously given to us by getting to know, personally and intimately, the One who invited us to God. The best invitation we ever received! We were also given absolutely terrific promises to pass on to you—your tickets to participation in the life of God after you turned your back on a world corrupted by lust.
>
> 2 Peter 1:3–4 THE MESSAGE

The purpose of salvation is not simply to avoid hell (though let's not minimize this benefit!). No, it is "to glorify God, and to *enjoy* him forever."[14] It is to share, by grace alone, in the light and love of God as his adopted children. It's what the New Testament calls being "in Christ" and in the Holy Trinity, as we see in the prayer that Jesus offered for all believers before his death:

> I pray also for those who will believe in me through their message, that all of them may be one, Father, just as you are in me and I am in you. May they also be in us....
> I in them and you in me....
> Father, I want those you have given me to be with me where I am, and to see my glory, the glory you have given me because you loved me before the creation of the world....
> I have made you known to them, and will continue to make you known in order that the love you have for me may be in them and that I myself may be in them.
>
> John 17:21, 23, 24, 26

Indeed, the best invitation ever!

Pelagians and Sufis

Throughout this book I've been speaking of Christianity and Islam in terms of their mainline, orthodox expressions. But this isn't the whole story. In both traditions there are heresies and sectarian movements that challenge and even contradict certain fundamental beliefs and aspects of spirituality. Thus it is that Pelagian Christians sometimes sound like Muslims when they talk about salvation and grace, while Sufi Muslims sometimes sound like Christians when they describe the love of God and the heart's desire to know him.

Muhammad probably never heard of Pelagius, an obscure monk from Ireland who became embroiled with Augustine in a bruising controversy over the nature of grace and the meaning of salvation. Pelagius became upset when he heard Augustine's prayer, "O Lord, give what you command, and command whatever you will." This prayer seemed to cut the moral nerve of the

Christian faith. If we were not able to obey God's commandments, then why had he given them in the first place?

Salvation, Pelagius said, came about by the performance of good works and the fulfillment of obligations laid down by God. If Augustine taught the doctrine of original sin, Pelagius believed in original uprightness. We don't need to be "born again," because we were born just fine the first time! If we do sin, God is ready to forgive, and we can reform ourselves by means of strenuous moral effort.

> *Sufi writings express so beautifully some of the deepest themes of biblical faith.*

What is grace then? To this way of thinking, grace is the guidance God has given in the law and in the prophets of the Old Testament and in the example of Jesus in the New. Together with this guidance and our own natural-born capacity to obey the law and to follow Jesus' example, we can achieve a right standing with God on our own. The Pelagians were incurable optimists, more so than the later Muslims, who did have a strong sense of the breach in the moral order brought about by sin. But their mutual analysis of the human situation and their belief in the possibility of self-salvation through obedience to external standards are strikingly similar.

The Sufis were Muslim mystics who may have been influenced by early Christian monks. They came to challenge certain assumptions of the orthodox Muslim tradition. Sufis are still regarded as heretics by certain Muslims who advocate a return to a strict observance of Islamic law, although the Sufis' influence and writings have been widely accepted by others.

Christians have long been attracted to Sufi writings because they express so beautifully some of the deepest themes of biblical faith, such as the love of God, the soul's yearning for God, and the need for God's grace. Like Solomon's Song of Songs in the Old Testament, the Sufi mystics often found in married love an analogy of God's love for us. An eighth-century woman saint, Rabi'a al-Adawiyya, has this in mind as she speaks her famous night prayer:

> My God and my Lord: Eyes are at rest, the stars are setting, hushed are the movements of birds in their nests, of monsters in the deep. And you are the Just who knows no change, the Equity that does not swerve, the Everlasting that never passes away. The doors of Kings are locked and guarded by their henchmen, but your door is open to those who call upon you. My Lord, each lover is now alone with his beloved. And I am alone with you.[15]

Another Muslim prayer expresses the sense of absolute dependence on God and the human need for forgiveness, grace, and assurance:

> Lo I thy servant am at thy door; thine abject one at thy door; thy captive at thy door; thy destitute one at thy door; thy client at thy door, oh Lord of the worlds. A weary one is at thy door, oh thou helper of them that seek for help. Thine anxious one is at thy door, oh thou who doest lift away the care of the careworn. And I, thy rebel, oh thou who seekest repentance, thy rebel who acknowledges his fault is at thy door. Oh thou who forgivest sinners, one who confesses his sin is at thy door. Oh most merciful of the merciful, he who has erred is at thy door. Oh Lord of the worlds, he who has wronged is at thy door. The lowly, fearful one is at thy door. Have mercy upon me, Lord.[16]

Can anyone who offers such a prayer be far from the heart of God? To all who lie, like this person, prostrate, exhausted, helpless at the door of the Lord of the worlds, that same Lord, even Jesus, says this: "Look at me. I stand at the door. I knock. If you hear me call and open the door, I'll come right in and sit down to supper with you" (Revelation 3:20 THE MESSAGE).

CHAPTER SEVEN

TRUTH TO TELL

Here is a trustworthy saying that deserves full acceptance: Christ Jesus came into the world to save sinners—of whom I am the worst.

PAUL, IN 1 TIMOTHY 1:15

As long as Christ is Christ, and the church knows both itself and him, there will be a mission to Islam. We present Christ for the sole, sufficient reason that he deserves to be presented. But we cannot neglect that Christ claims discipleship and that his gospel is something expecting a verdict.

KENNETH CRAGG

I first heard the name of Cat Stevens back in the early 1970s when I was a student at Harvard Divinity School and the pastor of a small inner-city church in Boston, Massachusetts. A number of young people in that community put their trust in Jesus as a result of the ministry of a Christian coffeehouse we had started. At that time Cat Stevens was at the height of his success as a pop star. The young people used to play his music. I remember well one of his songs from that period: "Morning has broken like the first morning. . . . Praise with elation, praise every morning. God's re-creation of the new day." Some of our young people thought Cat Stevens was a born-again Christian and that this song expressed his newfound faith in Jesus. More likely it expressed a deep yearning born out of spiritual hunger and out of a growing disillusionment with the nominal Christian faith he had grown up with—somewhat like another popular song of the times, George Harrison's "My sweet Lord. . . . I really want to know you, Lord."

For more than twenty years, Cat Stevens, now known as Yusuf Islam, has been a Muslim. In describing his journey to Islam, he describes his early religious upbringing and his puzzlement at the way the doctrine of the Trinity was presented to him:

> I looked at some of the statues of Jesus, they were just stones with no life. And when they said that God is three, I was puzzled even more but could not argue. . . . I was taught that God exists, but there was no direct contact with God, so we had to make contact with him through Jesus— he was in fact the door to God. This was more or less accepted by me, but I did not swallow it all.[1]

While Cat Stevens is a special case, many Christian young people grow up in similar circumstances. They attend church, perhaps become baptized, and may even participate in the exuberant activities of the church youth group. But somehow they remain distant from the reality of the Christian faith. For them the Trinity is a theological riddle to pay lip service to, not the profound reality of the living God at the heart of the universe. Jesus, too, is lifeless and far away, like the stone statues Cat Stevens saw and then walked away from. The greatest challenge facing the church today is determining how to pass on the faith intact to the rising generation. The resurgence of Islam in North America, as well as around the world, makes this challenge more urgent today than ever before.

In this concluding chapter, I want to review several of the foundational questions I've raised throughout this book in an effort to increase understanding of some of the major theological differences between Christianity and Islam. In doing so, I encourage you to resist the temptation to write off this kind of discussion as "just theology." Christianity without theology becomes a self-help philosophy or an empty moralism with no transcendent message. Every word of Paul's summary of the gospel in 1 Timothy 1:15 ("Christ Jesus came into the world to save sinners") is loaded theologically.

But theology is about more than doctrines, theories, and word studies. Theology affects *everything* we do— our prayer life, our family life, how we relate to our neighbors, our attitudes and motivations no less than our external actions. Puritan teacher William Ames insightfully observes, "Theology is the science of living in the presence of God." Islam, too, is an intensely theological religion. It makes definite, absolute claims about God, the world, and revelation. The fact that both Christianity and Islam take seriously these matters of ultimate concern means that a conversation between their adherents is possible.

> *The greatest challenge facing the church is determining how to pass on the faith intact to the rising generation.*

For 1400 years Christianity and Islam have shared a common, but uneasy, border—a border marked by animosity and one frequently stained with blood. This fact has made the Christian mission to Islam enormously difficult, despite the heroic work of missionary pioneers from Francis of Assisi to Kenneth Cragg. Perhaps out of the present world crisis will come a new openness to the Christian gospel in the Abode of Islam. In the spirit of Abraham's prayer long ago, surely Christians today should pray for such an openness: "And Abraham said to God, 'If only Ishmael might live under your blessing!'" (Genesis 17:18).

In the meantime, Christians who seek to bear a credible witness to Muslims will find indispensable the virtues of *patience* and *perseverance.* In 1 Timothy 1:15, Paul declared himself the worst of sinners and then went on to explain this dubious superlative as an occasion for others to see God's forbearance at work—"so that in me, the worst of sinners, Christ Jesus might display his unlimited patience as an example for those who would believe on him and receive eternal life" (1 Timothy 1:16). Indeed, Jesus has been patient not only with Paul but with all of us; otherwise we would have perished long ago (see 2 Peter 3:9). If Jesus is thus patient with us, what right do we have to be hasty and overbearing with others? Jesus rebuked his disciples when they threatened to call fire down from heaven to destroy certain Samaritans who didn't welcome their message (see Luke 9:52–56). But the other side of patience is perseverance, a willingness to be lovingly tenacious, to be steadfast in our witness despite difficulty and disappointment.

Patience and perseverance will help us avoid two approaches to Islam—neither of which is likely to advance the Christian gospel. The first approach majors on truth but lacks love; the second seeks to be loving but hedges on the truth. Throughout this book I've tried to avoid both extremes. The vilification of Islam and the denigration of Muhammad are well-established traditions in the literature of Christian polemics, going back to the Middle Ages. Christians have at times been drawn into debates with Muslims in the interest of defending the truth. But it is possible to win an argument and lose a soul. There may well be a place for Christian-Muslim debates, but in all such encounters we do well to remember the wise words of Henry Martyn, the great apostle to Islam in the early nineteenth century: "Oh that I could converse and reason, and plead, with power from on high. How powerless are the best-directed arguments, till the Holy Spirit renders them effectual."[2]

A second—and equally inadequate—approach to Islam assumes that all religions are essentially the same. Why worry about any particular differences? General pluralism, it is said, "recognizes not only the existence of other religions, but their intrinsic *equal value.*"[3] But, as I've noted throughout the book, the cavalier attitude toward truth adopted by this position does justice neither to Islamic theology nor to the Christian faith. By discounting the religious truth-claims of both Christianity and Islam, the pluralist position doesn't give an honest reading of either tradition and is disrespectful to both. With these cautions in mind, I want to take one more look at five central questions in illuminating the differences between Christianity and Islam.

Is the Father of Jesus the God of Muhammad?

There are some questions that do not allow for a simple yes or no answer, and this is one of them. The Father of Jesus is the only God there is, and in that sense he is the God of every person who has ever lived, including Muhammad. The Father of Jesus is the God Paul had in mind when Paul addressed the pagan Athenians on Mars Hill, "Now what you worship as something unknown I am going to proclaim to you" (Acts 17:23). Insofar as Muhammad was able to dispel the idols of Arabia and break through to an understanding of the one Creator God, the sustainer and judge of all the earth, he was doing something consistent with biblical faith. The God of the ninety-nine beautiful names—Glorious, Sovereign, Eternal, Mighty, Omniscient, Merciful, Sublime, and so forth—sounds very much like the God of Abraham, Isaac, and Jacob revealed in the Bible. How could this be, since Muslims were not a part of God's covenantal history with Israel? There are two possibilities: (1) Abraham may have passed on to Ishmael and his descendants (one of whom was Muhammad) a knowledge of the one God who was worthy of worship, and (2) God has not left himself without a witness among all people through his general revelation in nature and in the human conscience (see Acts 14:17; Romans 1:19–20).

There are two key passages in Romans where Paul addresses the issue under consideration here. In Romans 3:29–30 he asks whether the God of the Jews is not the God of the Gentiles as well. His answer is clear: "Yes, of Gentiles too, since there is only one God." He goes on to say that there is only one way of justification for Jews and Gentiles alike—by faith, not by works. The

> *Christ Jesus, God's eternal Son, is the sole and sufficient Savior for all persons everywhere.*

same issue comes up again in Romans 10:12, where Paul stresses the fact that God is an equal opportunity redeemer and will save anyone who calls on his name: "For there is no difference between Jew and Gentile—*the same Lord is Lord of all* and richly blesses all who call on him" (emphasis added).

Only one God ... the same Lord ... Lord of all. Paul does not teach, however, that this one God has established multiple pathways of salvation. On the contrary, he stresses the importance of an explicit Christian witness to all people. How can they call on the Lord unless they believe, how can they believe unless they hear, how can they hear without a preacher, how can they preach unless they are sent? (See Romans 10:14–15.)

In reverse order, we have here the New Testament strategy for Christian evangelism and missions: sent, preached, heard, believed, called, saved. God has given his stamp of approval to this means of sharing the gospel. These are the ordinary means of grace. That the living Christ sometimes appears in visions and dreams to those who have never read the Bible or heard the Christian witness is well attested in the records of Christian conversion. No matter how God may choose to get the message through, however, the content is ever the same. Christ Jesus, God's eternal Son—crucified, risen, and reigning—is the sole and sufficient Savior for all persons everywhere.

But in another—and decisive—sense, the Father of Jesus is *not* the God of Muhammad, for Christians and Muslims have radically different understandings of the character and nature of God. Kenneth Cragg summarizes the difference in this way: "God in the Quran and God in Christ are God under seriously divergent criteria of Godness.... The concept of divine power as incompatible with an earth-dwelling enterprise is sharply contrasted with that of the gospel where Christ crucified *is* the power of God."[4]

While the acknowledgment of the one sovereign God is a significant advance over pagan idolatry, bare monotheism alone is not enough. It yields a God who is a unit, not a unity. It gives us a deity that is infinite but not personal. On the basis of general revelation alone, some of the Greek philosophers had recognized the folly of idolatry and had professed faith in the one God long before Muhammad.

This is far different from the dynamic monotheism of both the Old and New Testaments. There God is revealed as the one who communicates himself—not just his will—to his people. He is *Elohim,* the Lord of Hosts who protects and defends his people. He is *El Shaddai,* the holy God who condemns sins. He is *Yahweh,* the covenant God of love and mercy. His oneness is not a numerical unity, for that would be to reduce God to a thing. Rather, it is a rich unity of relationship and love. As God says to his people through the prophet Haggai, " 'For I am with you,' declares the LORD Almighty. 'This is what I covenanted with you when you came out of Egypt. And my Spirit remains among you. Do not fear' " (Haggai 2:4–5).

This is the God the New Testament teaches us to know as the Father of Jesus. He is the God who was "reconciling the world to himself in Christ" (2 Corinthians 5:19). He is God with us and God for us for all eternity. For this reason, we cannot say that Christians and Muslims worship the same God without qualifying biblically what we mean by *same* and what we mean by *God.*

Why Can't We Just Forget about the Trinity?

Not long ago a popular evangelical Christian leader devised a program of diet and exercise for Christian women that included a Bible study component. She was criticized for teaching certain things about the Trinity that were contrary to the orthodox Christian view. In responding to her critics, she declared that Christian women "don't care about the Trinity. What the women want is weight loss." Sadly, her statement has the ring of truth about it, not only for women who participate in weight-loss programs but for large sectors of the evangelical community. But the conversation with Islam makes discussion of (and therefore interest in) the Trinity unavoidable. If we don't bring it up, they will! The Quran (wrongly) accuses Christians of tritheism, and this charge is repeated and believed by millions of Muslims around the world.

The doctrine of the Trinity does not deny but rather reinforces the true unity of God. Christians do not worship a triad of the Father, the Virgin Mary, and Jesus. Insofar as the Quran rejects all notions of God's producing an offspring through sexual procreation, Christians can only express emphatic agreement. Nothing in the Bible or in any orthodox Christian tradition supports such a ridiculous mythology. The doctrine of the Trinity is about something else. It tells us that within the being of God himself there is a mysterious *living love*—a dynamic relationship of surrender and affirmation, of giving and receiving—among the Father, the Son, and the Holy Spirit. While God is supremely transcendent, he is not utterly alone. The Maker of heaven and earth is at once the triune God of holiness and love.

This is a difficult notion for Islam to accept. Like the God of Arius in the early church, the God of Islam does not disclose his innermost being to others. For both Arius and Islam, God is essentially unknowable and incommunicable. He is isolated and aloof in his omnipotence.

The Father of Jesus Christ is a different kind of God. His ultimate reality is not expressed in terms of brute power and solitary force. Though his sovereignty and absolute power are never in question, these are not the most decisive marks of God's divinity. What makes God God is the relationship of total and mutual self-giving by which the Father gives everything to the Son, and the Son offers back all that he has to glorify the Father, the love of each being established and sealed by the Holy Spirit, who proceeds from both. Long ago, Gregory of Nyssa put it this way: "It is not the vastness of the heavens and the bright shining of the constellations, the order of the universe and the unbroken administration over all existence, that so manifestly displays the transcendent power of God as his condescension to the weakness of our human nature, in the way sublimity is seen in lowliness."[5]

How do we know that the Trinity is true? We cannot deduce this teaching from philosophical speculation, psychological introspection, or general revelation. Only in Jesus Christ do we see clearly into the heart of God. It's why Jesus could say so boldly, "I am in the Father and the Father is in me" (John 14:11). And again, "Trust in God; trust

> *Only in Jesus Christ do we see clearly into the heart of God.*

also in me" (John 14:1). The reality of the Father's love displayed in the life, death, and resurrection of Jesus is made present to us here and now through the Holy Spirit.

The conversation with Islam affords evangelicals an opportunity to revisit the doctrine of the Trinity. Throughout the history of the church, believers have occasionally focused on one member of the divine Godhead to the virtual exclusion of the other two. Certain forms of liberal theology extol the fatherhood of God but (like Islam) reduce Jesus to the status of a prophet and regard the Holy Spirit as an impersonal force. There is also a kind of "Jesusanity" that ignores the Son's relationship to the Father and the Holy Spirit. And there have been "Spirit movements" in the church that emphasize ecstatic spiritual experiences, with little thought given to the purpose of the Father and the mission of the Son. The long history of misunderstanding over the Trinity between Christianity and Islam should alert us to the dangers that are inherent when the doctrine of the Trinity is neglected or misconstrued.

Do the Quran and the Bible Come from the Same Source?

Both Christianity and Islam are religions of revelation. They teach that God has revealed his will to human beings, that he has done so through apostles and prophets, and that this revelation has resulted in holy books that are to be believed and obeyed as the very Word of God. But here the similarity ends. Muslims believe that the Quran is a timeless, eternal book recorded in heaven on an imperishable tablet (85:21). Through the angel Gabriel God "sent down" this perfect revelation and gave it to his chosen messenger, Muhammad, a man who could not read or write. He was told to recite what he had heard. Others who heard his recitations (which came to him over several decades) remembered them and wrote them down in what we now know as the Quran. The Quran was given to Muhammad in Arabic, and Muslims believe that only the Arabic version of the Quran is the divinely approved and authoritative word of God.

How different the Christian understanding of biblical revelation! While many Christians believe in the verbal inspiration of the Bible (the doctrine that the words as well as the ideas and concepts were inspired by God), the words themselves are intrinsically related to events. In the Old Testament, these words record and reflect the mighty acts of God in the history of Israel. In the New Testament, they bear witness to the supreme event of the Incarnation (see John 5:39). On the other hand, the Quran reads like an assortment of instructions and advice not specifically tied to any historical event, although Muslims scholars do try to reconstruct "occasions of revelation" for specific *surahs*. The Bible, however, is one interconnected story told in sixty-six separate installments. The story line is carried from the law and the prophets through the historians and the psalmists to the evangelists and the apostles. The great acts of salvation history are tied to specific events in space and time: "In the year that King Uzziah died" (Isaiah 6:1); "In those days Caesar Augustus issued a decree" (Luke 2:1); "When Pontius Pilate was governor of Judea" (Luke 3:1). The Bible is the inspired record of what God has said and done in space and time, not the transcript of a timeless tablet preserved in heaven.

The sheer diversity of the Bible—its many genres and multiple authors—causes some Muslims to question its authority. Why are there four gospels instead of one? How did a personal letter Paul dashed off in a Roman jail make it into the Bible? But Christians see these human features of the Bible as evidence of the way God inspired his Word. He spoke not only *to* his messengers but also *through* them. Matthew could not have written Isaiah, nor could Paul have written Deuteronomy. God spoke through the personality and unique circumstances of each biblical writer in order to convey his will to his people. There are no psalms or lamentations in the Quran. These forms of expression involve suffering and sometimes even doubt on the part of God's messengers, and yet they are no less inspired than other portions of Scripture.

The Quran does speak of the Law, the Psalms, and the Gospel as divine revelations transmitted through Moses, David, and Jesus. But Muslim theology also teaches that these prior Scriptures have been corrupted and are no longer trustworthy. (A similar claim was made by Marcion and other Gnostic teachers who rejected the canonical books of the Bible and devised their own Scriptures in the early church.) One of the greatest ways to present the message of Jesus Christ to Muslims is to encourage them to read the Bible for themselves. The Holy Spirit uses the Bible to overcome prejudice and unbelief, as many Muslims who have become Jesus-followers attest:

> Far from remaining "a dead letter," the Bible often seems to operate like a living thing. There are those who begin to read it in order to find ammunition against Christianity, but sooner or later the Scripture pierces their armor and knocks on the door of their heart with God's eternal question: "And you, how are you responding to this summons?"[6]

What's So Crucial about the Cross?

When John 3:16 says that "God so loved the world that he gave his one and only Son," this "giving" refers not only to Jesus' birth, life, teachings, and miracles but also to his sacrificial death on the cross. The cross was not an accident. Jesus himself interpreted his suffering and death as the fulfillment of God's purpose to redeem human beings estranged from God by their sin. "Did not the Christ have to suffer these things and then enter his glory?" the risen Jesus asked his disciples on the road to Emmaus (Luke 24:26). Through his work on the cross, Jesus turned aside the wrath of God, absorbing the punishment due sinners, securing forgiveness and a right standing before God for all who trust in him. The Bible describes Jesus' finished work on the cross not only as a settling of accounts in heaven but also as a triumphant victory over all the powers of darkness.

> *The Bible describes Jesus' finished work on the cross as a triumphant victory over all the powers of darkness.*

But all of this is smoke and mirrors according to Islam. The crucifixion never happened. Jesus was raptured to heaven, and a substitute (perhaps Judas) was nailed to the cross in his place. Thus what Christians see as the means for the world's redemption, Islam regards as a charade.

Muslims were not the first to reject the Christian message of the cross. Around the year A.D. 180, the pagan philosopher Celsus published an attack against Christianity that anticipated the Muslim objection to the cross: "You will be a laughing stock so long as you repeat the blasphemy that the gods of other men are idols, while you brazenly worship as God a man whose life was wretched, who is known to have died (in disgraceful circumstances) and who, so you teach, is the very model of the God we should look to as our Father."[7]

The cross is shocking because it forces us to redefine our preconceived notions of who God is. Is he the kind of God who would deliberately deliver his Son over to this kind of fate? There are many ways to try to escape the scandal of the cross. Some, like Celsus, ridicule it. Muslims deny that it ever happened. The Ku Klux Klan burn it and use it as a pretext for their racist violence. Many Christians try to domesticate it by turning it into a piece of jewelry or a symbol on a steeple. But none of these denials and perversions can rob the cross of its power—which is really God's power—to reconcile lost sinners to God and to restore them to a relationship with him that brings pardon and peace, acceptance and access, and adoption into God's family.

These themes are reflected in two classic prayers of the Christian church. The first is the prayer of consecration from the sixteenth-century *Book of Common Prayer*: "Almighty God, our heavenly Father, who of thy tender mercy didst give thine only Son Jesus Christ to die upon the cross for our salvation, who made there, by his one oblation of himself once offered, a full, perfect and sufficient sacrifice, and satisfaction for the sins of the whole world . . ." The second is a simple affirmation from an ancient Syrian liturgy: "The Lord hath reigned from the tree."

What Must I Do to Be Saved?

The Quran teaches that God does (on occasion) love, forgive, and show mercy, but these acts are conditioned upon human obedience and response to his guidance. Sin in Islam is a kind of forgetfulness, or ignorance, which can be remedied through the "remembrance" of God's will revealed in the Quran. Because Islam is not a religion of redemption, there is no need for the cross and no place for grace.

The Christian diagnosis of the human condition is more radical than that of Islam. Humanity's problem is not merely ignorance but rebellion. Human beings are born as rebels against God by reason of original sin. Yet we cannot blame our sin on Adam or on anyone else, for "all have sinned and fall short of the glory of God" (Romans 3:23). Even Muslims recognize the universal waywardness of human beings. Idolatry is pervasive, and people must constantly be warned against *shirk*. The Bible teaches that the human condition is desperate and that all of our efforts to find God through strenuous moral endeavor *(jihad)* will come to naught. We must be born again—reshaped from within—by the power of the Holy Spirit.

Abdiyah Akbar Abdul-Haqq spent many years sharing the gospel with Muslims as a partner with the Billy Graham Evangelistic Association. He recognized the need that all human beings have for acceptance, forgiveness, and grace: "The only prescription for a spiritually meaningful life is redemption from sin and rehabilitation and fellowship with God Most High. But this is something beyond the power of the natural man who is so miserably stuck in the quicksand of sin that the more he tries to extricate himself the deeper he sinks. Salvation is possible only with God."[8]

Muslims scholars sometimes apply the parable Jesus told about the workers in the vineyard (see Matthew 20:1–16) to the three religions stemming from Abraham. According to this interpretation, the workers who go early in the morning represent Judaism, the noonday shift stands for Christianity, and those who start late in the day symbolize Islam. In this way, Islam comes out on top as God's final revelation.

In reality, the parable is about something quite different. The fact that the stragglers who were hired right before closing were paid the same amount as everyone else is a picture of God's unmerited and surprising grace. Those who had toiled all day in the sun were naturally furious. "We deserve much more than these Johnny-come-latelies!" they might have exclaimed in today's terminology. They were amazed—and pretty upset—at the generosity of the vineyard's owner toward these ill-deserving workers. The disgruntled workers' argument makes perfect sense for those who assume they can relate to God on a quid pro quo basis. But the message of the parable turns all religions of good works upside down. The fact that God calls us at all is a matter of sheer grace, his freely given favor. If God blesses us with good things, including salvation, it is *not* because of the hours worked, the effort expended, the merits earned. It is all grace—grace undeserved!

> *The fact that God calls us at all is a matter of sheer grace.*

A Final Prayer

If theology is the science of living in the presence of God, it is appropriate to conclude this book by calling on God, the one Jesus taught us to call "our Father in heaven." Let us join our hearts with the words of the prayer offered by Samuel Zwemer at the Keswick Convention in 1915: "O God, to whom the Muslim world bows in homage five times daily, look in mercy upon its people and reveal to them thy Christ."

As we pray for Muslims, so we pray for ourselves, that we, too, may know Jesus Christ, whom to know truly is life eternal. May God grant us the courage and the wisdom to proclaim the cross in the spirit of him who bore it. May we show by word and deed how wide and long and high and deep is the love of Christ. And may

Glory be to the Father and to the Son and to the Holy Spirit;
as it was in the beginning, is now and ever shall be,
world without end!
Amen.

The Nicene Creed

We believe in one God,
the Father, the Almighty,
maker of heaven and earth,
of all that is, seen and unseen.

We believe in one Lord, Jesus Christ,
the only Son of God,
eternally begotten of the Father,
God from God, Light from Light,
true God from true God,
begotten, not made,
of one being with the Father.
Through him all things were made.
For us and for our salvation
   he came down from heaven;
by the power of the Holy Spirit
   he became incarnate from the Virgin Mary,
   and was made man.
For our sake he was crucified under Pontius Pilate;
he suffered death and was buried.
On the third day he rose again
   in accordance with the Scriptures;
he ascended into heaven,
   and is seated at the right hand of the Father.
He will come again in glory
   to judge the living and the dead,
   and his kingdom will have no end.

We believe in the Holy Spirit, the Lord, the giver of life,
who proceeds from the Father and the Son.
With the Father and the Son
   he is worshiped and glorified.
He has spoken through the Prophets.
We believe in one holy catholic and apostolic Church.
We acknowledge one baptism for the forgiveness of sins.
We look for the resurrection of the dead,
and the life of the world to come. Amen. *

**The Nicene Creed (modern wording).*

FOR FURTHER READING

Braswell, George W. *What You Need to Know About Islam and Muslims.* Nashville: Broadman, 2000.

    A brief but clearly written overview of Islam by a Christian scholar who formerly taught on the faculty of Islamic Theology at the University of Tehran, Iran. Braswell's longer introduction is also worthy of note: *Islam: Its Prophet, Peoples, Politics and Power* (Nashville: Broadman, 1996).

Chapman, Colin. *Cross and Crescent: Responding to the Challenge of Islam.* Leicester: Inter-Varsity Press, 1993.

    A helpful review of the history of Islam and its culture and beliefs, with special emphasis on the spiritual and theological issues Christians face in sharing the gospel with Muslims.

Cragg, Kenneth. *The Call of the Minaret.* Oxford: Oneworld, 2000.

    First published in 1956, this highly acclaimed study by Bishop Kenneth Cragg has become a classic in Muslim-Christian relations. Among Cragg's many books, the following are highly recommended: *Sandals at the Mosque* (New York: Oxford Univ. Press, 1959); and *Jesus and the Muslim* (Oxford: Oneworld, 1999).

Dawood, N. J. *The Koran.* New York: Penguin Books, 1956.

    A highly literate, readable translation of the Quran in contemporary English. This translation is also available in a parallel English-Arabic edition published by Penguin Books.

Fernando, Ajith. *Sharing the Truth in Love: How to Relate to People of Other Faiths*. Grand Rapids: Discovery House, 2001.
A theologically sound and culturally sensitive discussion of cross-cultural evangelism.

Gaudeul, Jean-Marie. *Called from Islam to Christ: Why Muslims Become Christians*. London: Monarch, 1999.
A fascinating account of the ways in which many Muslims from many different parts of the world have become believers in Jesus Christ.

Geisler, Norman L., and Abdul Saleeb. *Answering Islam*. Grand Rapids: Baker, 1993.
Perhaps the best one-volume apologetic response to Islam from an evangelical Christian perspective. The Muslim case is presented with fairness and the Christian response avoids caricature. A valuable resource for Christians who want to share their faith with Muslims.

George, Ron. *Issues and Insights into Church Planting in the Muslim World*. Crowborough: WIN, 2000.
Written with sensitivity and insight, this brief volume examines hindrances to global evangelization and church planting among Muslims.

Kateregga, Badru D., and David W. Shenk. *A Muslim and a Christian in Dialogue*. Scottdale, Pa.: Herald, 1997.
A straightforward presentation of the major theological differences between Christianity and Islam, written by two colleagues, one a Christian and the other a Muslim who have taught together at Kenyatta University College in Kenya.

Murata, Sachiko, and William C. Chittick. *The Vision of Islam*. New York: Paragon, 1994.
A superb examination of the Muslim faith that draws on the Quran and accepted traditions of Islam. This book has been highly acclaimed by Islamic scholars as one of the best introductions to Muslim theology published in the West.

Musk, Bill. *The Unseen Face of Islam*. Crowborough: MARC, 1989.
This book's subtitle ("Sharing the Gospel with Ordinary Muslims") accurately describes the author's purpose: to present the real world in which millions of Muslims live, a world often at odds with official Islamic ideas and structures. This theme is further explored in another book by Bill Musk: *Touching the Soul of Islam* (Crowborough: MARC, 1995).

Parshall, Phil. *The Cross and the Crescent*. Wheaton, Ill.: Tyndale House, 1989.

This book incorporates insights from both Muslim scholars and Christian missiologists. Parshall seeks to understand the mind and heart of Islam from the perspective of a Christian who has lived and worked among Muslims for many years. See also two other books by Parshall: *New Paths in Muslim Evangelism* (Grand Rapids: Baker 1980) and *Inside the Community* (Grand Rapids: Baker, 1994).

Sardar, Ziauddin, and Zafar Abbas Malik. *Introducing Muhammad*. New York: Totem Books, 1994.

A popular presentation of Muhammad from an Islamic perspective. Well illustrated and informative.

Sheikh, Bilquis, with Richard H. Schneider. *I Dared to Call Him Father*. Grand Rapids: Baker, 1978.

Written by a Pakistani woman of noble birth who came to faith in Jesus through a series of dreams and through reading the Bible. Her story illustrates the harassment and persecution often experienced by Muslims who become Christ-followers.

Shorrosh, Anis A. *Islam Revealed*. Nashville: Nelson, 1988.

Written by a Palestinian-born Arab Christian evangelist known for his debates with the popular Muslim apologist Ahmed Daedet.

Woodberry, J. Dudley, ed. *Muslims and Christians on the Emmaus Road*. Monrovia, Calif.: MARC, 1989.

A collection of excellent essays written by leading scholars and missiologists who examine crucial issues in Christian witness among Muslims.

Zebiri, Kate. *Muslims and Christians Face to Face*. Oxford: Oneworld, 1997.

A helpful resource that examines both Muslim perspectives on Christianity and Christian literature on Islam.

Zwemer, Samuel M. *The Muslim Christ*. London: Oliphant Anderson and Ferrier, 1912.

Zwemer was a great missionary-scholar who died in 1952 after many years of Christian witness in the Muslim world. He was a prolific author, and his many writings, including this one, can still be read profitably.

GLOSSARY OF KEY TERMS

Allah—The Arabic word for God. Probably derived from *il ilah*, "the god." Arabic Christians addressed God as Allah long before Muhammad was born. Allah was used by pre-Islamic pagans to designate a notable deity in their religious system. Muhammad repudiated these pagan and polytheistic meanings when he declared, "There is no god but Allah."

Allahu akbar—"Allah is most great." A part of the daily call to prayer sounded from minarets around the world.

Caliph—The title of the successors of Muhammad. The first caliph, Abu Bakr, took office after Muhammad's death. The question of who should succeed Muhammad became a source of division between Sunni and Shiite Muslims. The office of caliph came to an end in 1924 with the fall of the Ottoman Turks.

Fatihah—The first chapter of the Quran. This prayer, which asks God for guidance to follow "the straight path," is repeated by Muslims each day during the five required prayers.

Fatwa—A legal opinion or expert ruling on some aspect of Islamic law.

Hadith—Literally, "story." This word refers to the sayings and deeds of the prophet Muhammad that were remembered by his companions and passed on to later generations. Eventually these sayings were brought together in a number of collections, six of which are regarded as authoritative by orthodox Islam.

Hajj—The Great Pilgrimage to Mecca. All Muslims are required to make this pilgrimage at least once during their lifetime, as long as health and financial means allow. The last month in the Muslim calendar is designated as the official time for the pilgrimage to Mecca, although it may be done at other times of the year as well. While in Mecca, Muslims perform various rituals, including walking around the *Kabah* and kissing the sacred Black Stone contained in its south wall.

Halal—That which is lawful or permitted according to Islamic law. This word also refers to meat that has been properly butchered in a kosherlike manner, with the animal's throat slit, its blood drained out, and its head turned to face Mecca.

Hanifs—A somewhat obscure group of pre-Islamic monotheists who found their way to the worship of the one God despite the idolatrous culture in which they lived. Muslims regard Abraham himself as one of the *Hanifs*. The mission of Muhammad was to restore the worship of the one God observed by Abraham and others in times past.

Hijrah—The "flight" of Muhammad and the early Muslim community from Mecca to Medina in A.D. 622. This event has been compared to the exodus in Judaism. It marked the beginning of the first Muslim *ummah* and the emergence of Muhammad as a political and military, as well as religious, leader. The year 622 marks the beginning of the Islamic calendar, as seen in the abbreviation A.H., after *hijrah*.

Iblis—The name for Satan in the Quran. Iblis, like the other *jinn*, or evil spirits, was created by God out of a fiery substance. Like the devil in Christian theology, he tempts human beings and seeks to thwart God's divine purpose in history.

Imam—A religious leader in Islam. This word usually refers to the person who leads prayers and presents teachings in the mosque. Shiite Muslims speak of the *imam* in a special sense as a divinely appointed ruler of the entire Muslim community.

Isa ibn Maryam—Jesus, son of Mary. The Quran refers to Jesus as a prophet and Messiah and records his virgin birth and miracles. However, Muslim theology denies both the Incarnation and the crucifixion. Muslims believe that Jesus was raptured to heaven, while an unknown substitute (perhaps Judas) was put to death in his place on the cross.

Jihad—The obligation of Muslims to struggle or exert themselves "in the way of the Lord," for the furtherance of Islam in their own lives and around the world. Islamic tradition distinguished *jihad* of the heart from *jihad* of the sword. The latter, also called "the lesser *jihad*," may be considered a form of holy war.

Kabah—Literally, "cube." Once a pagan shrine, the *Kabah* is the central sanctuary of Islam. All Muslims bow toward the *Kabah* when they offer daily prayers to God. This cubelike structure is also the focus of the required pilgrimage to Mecca.

Kufr—A deliberate concealing or hiding from the light of God. This word is synonymous with unbelief and the denial of God's revelation.

Mihrab—The niche in the wall of a mosque pointing in the direction of the *Kabah* in Mecca. In the Middle Ages, the compass was developed by Muslims to help determine the most accurate angle for directing their prayers to Mecca.

Minaret—The tower attached to a mosque from which the daily call to prayer is sounded.

Mosque—A building set aside for public prayer. Muslim men gather in the mosque for prayer each Friday.

Mushrik—One who is guilty of committing *shirk*. An idolater.

Muslim—One who practices *islam,* or surrender to God. In this sense, Jesus is called a *muslim* in the Quran. Since the time of Muhammad, this word has referred to those who accept the revelation of the Quran and who practice the Five Pillars of the Islamic faith.

Nabi—Prophet. A messenger who brings guidance from God for the human race. God is said to have sent 124,000 prophets in all from Adam to Muhammad. The Quran records the names of twenty-five prophets, including Moses, David, and Jesus.

Quran—The name of the holy book of Islam, meaning "recital." For Muslims, the Quran is the supreme revelation of God corresponding to Jesus Christ in the Christian faith. The Quran is the authoritative word of God only in Arabic, the language in which it was revealed to Muhammad through the angel Gabriel.

Ramadan—The ninth month of the year in the Islamic calendar. During this month Muslims are expected to fast from dawn until sunset. Muslims believe that the first revelation of the Quran came to Muhammad during this month in the year A.D. 610.

Rasul—Apostle or messenger. A *rasul* is a special kind of prophet who brings a distinctive revelation from God often recorded in a book. Moses, Jesus, and Muhammad are three prophets who fulfilled this role.

Salat—The act of ritual prayer Muslims are required to offer to Allah five times each day. Muslims wash their hands and feet before prostrating themselves toward Mecca for these prayers. Muslim men are required to attend the public prayers offered each Friday in the mosque.

Sawm—Fasting. A spiritual discipline that may be performed at any time during the year but is required of devout Muslims during Ramadan.

Shahada—The confession that "there is no god but God and Muhammad is the Messenger [Prophet] of God." The first and most basic of the Five Pillars of Islam. By reciting the *Shahada* with sincerity, in the presence of two or more witnesses, one becomes a Muslim.

Shariah—Literally, "the road or path leading to water." This term denotes the holy law of God in Islam. The *shariah* is based on the Quran—its commandments, inferences, and implications— as interpreted by various legal traditions in Islam. How the *shariah* should be applied within a given society is a matter of debate among Muslims, but there is a strong call throughout the Islamic world for the strict observance of Quranic law in Muslim societies.

Shirk—The one unforgivable sin in Islam. Those who are guilty of *shirk* confuse the Creator with the creature by associating something that is not divine with God. Muslims believe Christians are guilty of *shirk* when they worship Jesus as the divine Son of God.

Sufi—A Muslim mystic. This word comes from *suf* ("wool"), indicating the rough clothing worn by the early mystics, whose lifestyle may have been influenced by Christian monks. Sufism expresses a longing to know and love God in a personal way. Some strict Muslims regard Sufis as unorthodox and outside the pale of Islam, but most Sufis consider themselves to be faithful followers of the orthodox Islamic faith.

Surah—A chapter of the Quran. This word literally means "fence" or "enclosure." There are 114 *surahs* in the Quran, arranged in the order of descending length. Each *surah* is divided into verses (called *ayat*).

Tawhid—The affirmation of God's essential oneness and unity. The first formula of the *Shahada* expresses this basic tenet of Islam.

Ummah—The worldwide Muslim community, also referred to as the Abode of Islam. In theory, the caliph is the earthly head of the *ummah*. Since the fall of the Ottoman Turks in 1924, however, the office of caliph has been vacant in Islam.

Zakat—The required giving of alms. Each Muslim is expected to contribute 2.5 percent of his or her annual income for the maintenance of the Muslim community and the relief of the poor and needy.

NOTES

Preface

1. Thomas Merton, *Seeds of Contemplation* (New York: New Directions Publications, 1949), 17.

2. Timothy George, "Is the God of Muhammad the Father of Jesus?" *Christianity Today,* 4 February 2002, 28–35.

3. N. J. Dawood, translator, *The Koran,* 7th rev. ed. (New York: Penguin Classics, 2000).

Introduction

1. Cited in Jaroslav Pelikan, *Jesus Through the Centuries* (New York: Harper & Row, 1985), 299, emphasis added.

2. W. E. Hocking, *Living Religions and a World Faith* (New York: Macmillan, 1940), 231.

3. See Jean-Marie Gaudeul, *Called from Islam to Christ: Why Muslims Become Christians* (London: Monarch, 1999).

4. Simone Weil, *Waiting for God* (San Francisco: Harper & Row, 1973), 69.

Chapter One: What Is Islam?

1. See Ron George, *Issues and Insights into Church Planting in the Muslim World* (Crowborough: WIN, 2000), 7–13.

2. United Nations Population Division, *World Population Prospects: The 1992 Revisions* (New York: United Nations, 1993), table A18.

3. Cited in Bruce A. McDowell and Anees Zaka, *Muslims and Christians at the Table* (Phillipsburg, N.J.: P&R Publishing, 1999), 4.

4. Allen Sipress, "Keeping Faith in Growing Numbers," *Philadelphia Inquirer*, 25 July 1993, A-10.

5. George, *Church Planting in the Muslim World*, 4.

6. Bill Musk, *The Unseen Face of Islam: Sharing the Gospel with Ordinary Believers* (East Sussex: MARC Evangelical Missionary Alliance, 1989).

7. Cited in Kenneth Cragg and Marston Speight, *Islam from Within: Anthology of a Religion* (Belmont, Calif.: Wadsworth, 1980), 48.

8. Kenneth Cragg, ed., *Readings in the Qur'an* (London: Harper-Collins, 1988), 84.

9. Syed Muhammad al-Naquib al-attas, "Islam: The Concept of Religion and the Foundation of Ethics and Morality," in *The Challenge of Islam*, ed. Altaf Gauhar (London: Islamic Council of Europe, 1978), 48.

10. See Frank Peters, "The Quest for the Historical Muhammad," *International Journal of Middle East Studies*, 23 (1991): 291–313.

11. W. Montgomery Watt, *Early Islam* (Edinburgh: Edinburgh Univ. Press, 1990), ix.

12. See Charles Kimball, *Striving Together: A Way Forward in Christian-Muslim Relations* (Maryknoll, N.Y.: Orbis, 1991), 40–41; Norman Daniel, *Islam and the West: The Making of an Image* (Oxford: One World, 1993). On the various ways Muhammad has been seen over the centuries, see Gabriel Said Reynolds, "Muhammad Through Christian Eyes," *Books and Culture*, 8/1 (2001): 6–8.

13. Norman L. Geisler and Abdul Saleeb, *Answering Islam: The Crescent in the Light of the Cross* (Grand Rapids: Baker, 1993).

14. Charles Kraft, *Christianity in Cross-Cultural Perspective: A Study in Dynamic Biblical Theologizing* (Maryknoll, N.Y.: Orbis, 1981), 402.

15. See Colin Chapman, *Cross and Crescent* (Leicester: Inter-Varsity Press, 1995), 233.

Chapter Two: Ties That Bind, Scars That Hurt

1. Cited in Sachiko Murata and William C. Chittick, *The Vision of Islam* (New York: Paragon, 1994), 202.

2. Ruth Tucker, *From Jerusalem to Irian Jaya: A Biographical History of Christian Missions* (Grand Rapids: Zondervan, 1993), 23.

3. Bernard of Clairvaux, "Why You Should Crusade," *Christian History* 12/4 (1993): 18.

4. Steven Runciman, *A History of the Crusades* (Harmondsworth: Penguin, 1965), 3:480.

5. Richard John Neuhaus, "The Approaching Century of Religion," *First Things* 76 (October 1997): 79.

6. Cited in Lyle L. Vander Werff, *Christian Mission to Muslims* (Pasadena: William Carey Library, 1977), 13–14. In an ironic twist of history, Muslim aggression against Europe in the sixteenth century enabled Luther's Reformation to survive. Because his attention was diverted by the Ottoman Turks, the Catholic emperor Charles V could not wage an effective war against the Protestant princes of Germany.

7. "The Rule of 1221," in *St. Francis of Assisi: English Omnibus of the Sources for the Life of St. Francis* (Chicago: Franciscan Herald Press, 1973), 43–44.

8. See Kenneth Cragg, *The Call of the Minaret* (Maryknoll, N.Y.: Orbis, 1985), 221.

Chapter Three: Is the Father of Jesus the God of Muhammad?

1. Samuel Zwemer, on the other hand, argued that Muhammad had ample opportunity to learn what orthodox believers thought about the Trinity and that he deliberately rejected the Christian idea of the Godhead. See Zwemer's *The Moslem Doctrine of God* (Boston: American Tract Society, 1905), 80–92.

2. Saint Augustine, *Quaestiones in Heptateuchum*, 2/73; PL34, 632.

Chapter Four: Why the Trinity Matters

1. Carl F. H. Henry, *God, Revelation and Authority* (Waco, Tex.: Word, 1982), 5:171.

2. See Kenneth Cragg, *Muhammad and the Christian* (Maryknoll, N.Y.: Orbis, 1984), 124–25.

3. Bilquis Sheikh, *I Dared to Call Him Father* (Grand Rapids: Chosen Books, 1978).

4. Cited in Wilhelm Pauck, ed., *Melanchthon and Bucer* (Philadelphia: Westminster, 1969), 21.

5. The Nicene Creed (traditional wording).

6. Cited in Arthur C. McGill, *Suffering: A Test of Theological Method* (Philadelphia: Westminster, 1982), 70. I owe my interpretation of Arius and his role in the Trinitarian controversy to McGill, one of my former teachers at Harvard Divinity School. His untimely death in 1980 left the world bereft of a brilliant theologian.

7. McGill, *Suffering*, 76.

8. John Milton, *Samson Agonistes*, lines 472–78.

9. See the treatment of this theme in Norman Anderson, *God's Law and God's Love* (London: Collins, 1980), 74–104. The conditional nature of God's love is further explained in a famous *hadith* from later Islamic tradition: "My servant draws near to Me by means of nothing dearer to Me than that which I have established as a duty for him. And My servant continues drawing nearer to Me through supererogatory acts *until* I love him; and when I love him, I become his ear with which he hears, his eye with which he sees, his hand with which he grasps, and his foot with which he walks. And if he asks Me [for something] I give it to him. If indeed he seeks My help, I help him" (emphasis mine). On the interpretation of this *hadith,* see William Graham, *Divine Word and Prophetic Word in Early Islam* (The Hague: Mouton, 1975), 173.

10. Cragg, *Muhammad and the Christian*, 103.

11. The Jewish midrash is recounted in Pinchas Lapide and Jürgen Moltmann, *Jewish Monotheism and Christian Trinitarian Doctrine* (Philadelphia: Fortress, 1981), 65. An example of a popular Christian version of this theme is found in James Weldon Johnson, *God's Trombones* (New York: Viking, 1948).

12. Cited in Seyyed Hossein Nasr, *Islamic Spirituality* (New York: Crossroad, 1987), 321.

13. Karl Barth, *Church Dogmatics* IV/2, 755.

14. Thomas Hardy, "The Dynasts," in *The Works of Thomas Hardy in Prose and Verse* (London: Macmillan, 1913), 2:254. See the treatment of this theme in Peter Jensen, *At the Heart of the Universe* (Wheaton: Crossway, 1997), 75–94.

15. See Bruce J. Nicholls, "New Theological Approaches in Muslim Evangelism," in *The Gospel and Islam*, ed. Don M. McCurry (Monrovia, Calif.: MARC, 1979), 155–81.

16. John of Damascus, "Exposition of the Orthodox Faith," in *The Nicene and Post-Nicene Fathers*, 2nd series, 9:17.

17. McGill, *Suffering*, 82.

Chapter Five: Jesus with Freckles?

1. See Lesslie Newbigin, *The Finality of Christ* (London: SEM Press, 1969).

2. This is the first article of the Barmen Declaration. See John Leith, ed., *Creeds of the Churches*, 3rd ed. (Atlanta: John Knox, 1983), 520.

3. See Bernard Lewis, *Cultures in Conflict: Christians, Muslims, and Jews in the Age of Discovery* (New York: Oxford Univ. Press, 1995), 30–53.

4. John Paul II, *Crossing the Threshold of Hope* (New York: Knopf, 1994), 92–93, emphasis added.

5. For the views of Hesselgrave and Murad, see Kate Zebiri's *Muslims and Christians Face to Face* (Oxford: Oneworld, 1997), 43. While appreciative of the pope's acknowledgment of Islam as a living religious community, Hartford Seminary professor Ibrahim M. Abu-Rabi' is critical of the pope's theologically conservative Christian exclusivism. See his "Pope John Paul II and Islam," *The Muslim World* 88 (1998): 279–96.

6. Cited in Robert Payne, *The History of Islam* (New York: Dorset, 1959), 81.

7. Stories of Jesus making clay figures of animals and giving them life are recorded in several of the Apocryphal gospels. See Geoffrey Parrinder, *Jesus in the Quran* (New York: Oxford Univ. Press, 1977), 83–84.

8. Kenneth Cragg, *Jesus and the Muslim* (Oxford: Oneworld, 1999), 28.

9. E. Gulshan and Thelma Sangster, *The Torn Veil: Christ's Healing Power Breaks Through to a Muslim Girl* (Marshall, Morgan and Scott: Basingstoke, 1984). Fatima's story is also recounted in Jean-Marie Gaudeul, *Called from Islam to Christ* (East Sussex: Monarch Publications, 1999), 34–37.

10. Cited in Cragg, *Jesus and the Muslim*, 74, footnote 62.

11. Cited in Cragg, *Jesus and the Muslim*, 186. For the background of this text, see James M. Robinson, ed., *The Nag Hammadi Library* (New York: Harper & Row, 1977), 339–40.

12. Cited in Cragg, *Jesus and the Muslim*, 75.

13. Cited in John C. Wenger, ed., *The Complete Writings of Menno Simons* (Scottdale, Pa.: Herald, 1956), 621.

14. Lamin Sanneh, "Jesus, More Than a Prophet," in Kelly Monroe, ed., *Finding God at Harvard* (Grand Rapids: Zondervan, 1996), 192–94.

15. This poem was written by Edward Shillito after World War I. See William Temple's *Readings in St. John's Gospel* (London: Macmillan, 1942), 385.

Chapter Six: Grace for the Straight Path

1. Colin Chapman, "Biblical Foundations of Praying for Muslims," in J. Dudley Woodberry, ed., *Muslims and Christians on the Emmaus Road* (Monrovia, Calif.: MARC Publications, 1989), 313.

2. Ismail al-Faruqi, *Christian Ethics: A Historical and Systematic Analysis of Its Dominant Ideas* (Toronto: McGill Univ. Press, 1967), 202.

3. David L. Johnson, *A Reasoned Look at Asian Religions* (Minneapolis: Bethany House, 1985), 144–51.

4. Note this statement by the great Sufi scholar al-Ghazali: "Do not neglect your inner being, which lies at the heart of all purification. Endeavor to purify it with repentance and remorse for your excesses, and a determined resolution not to commit them in the future. Cleanse your inner being in this way, for that is the place to be examined by the One you worship." Cited in Phil Parshall, *The Cross and the Crescent* (Wheaton, Ill.: Tyndale House, 1989), 145–46.

5. Cited in Parshall, *The Cross and the Crescent*, 145.

6. See the treatment of this theme by Colin Chapman, "The God Who Reveals," in *Muslims and Christians on the Emmaus Road*, 127–44.

7. Abul A'la Maududi, "What Islam Stands For," in *The Challenge of Islam*, ed. Altaf Gauhar (London: Islamic Council of Europe, 1978), 12.

8. See Ida Glaser, "The Concept of Relationship as a Key to the Comparative Understanding of Christianity and Islam," *Themelios* 11/2 (January 1986): 57–60.

9. Glaser, "The Concept of Relationship," 58.

10. D. M. Baillie, *God Was in Christ* (New York: Charles Scribner's Sons, 1948), 175.

11. Cited in Jens Christensen, *The Practical Approach to Muslims* (London: North Africa Mission, 1977), 380.

12. Martin Luther, *A Commentary on St. Paul's Epistle to the Galatians*, ed. Phillip Watson (London: James Clarke and Co., 1953), 372.

13. This term was used by Ismail al-Faruqi, who also refers to the Christian "preoccupation" with the doctrine of original sin as "peccatism." See Kate Zebiri, *Muslims and Christians Face to Face* (Oxford: Oneworld, 1997), 149.

14. Westminster Shorter Catechism, Question and Answer 1.

15. Cited in Huston Smith, *The World's Religions* (San Francisco: HarperSanFrancisco, 1991), 260.

16. Cited in S. J. Samartha and J. B. Taylor, eds., *Christian-Muslim Dialogue: Papers Presented at the Broumana Consultation*, 12–18 July 1972 (Geneva: World Council of Churches, 1973), 114.

Chapter Seven: Truth to Tell

1. Yusuf Islam, "My Journey to Islam," Imperial College Islamic Society Web site, January 5, 2002.

2. Cited in Samuel Wilberforce, *Journals and Letters of Henry Martyn* (London: Seeley & Burnside, 1837), 2:373.

3. Hans Küng, *Christianity and World Religions* (Maryknoll, N.Y.: Orbis, 1993), 180, emphasis added.

4. Kenneth Cragg, *Sandals at the Mosque* (New York: Oxford Univ. Press, 1959), 91–92.

5. Gregory of Nyssa, *Oratio Catechetica Magna*, 24.

6. Jean-Marie Gaudeul, *Called from Islam to Christ* (East Sussex: Monarch Publications, 1999), 70.

7. Celsus, *On the True Doctrine: A Discourse Against the Christians,* trans. R. Joseph Hoffmann (New York: Oxford University Press, 1987), 110.

8. Abdiyah Akbar Abdul-Haqq, *Sharing Your Faith with a Muslim* (Minneapolis: Bethany House Publishers, 1980), 157.

We want to hear from you. Please send your comments about this book to us in care of the address below. Thank you.

GRAND RAPIDS, MICHIGAN 49530 USA

WWW.ZONDERVAN.COM